The Psychologist's Book
of Personality Tests

The Psychologist's Book of Personality Tests

24 Revealing Tests to Identify and Overcome Your Personal Barriers to a Better Life

Louis Janda, Ph.D.

John Wiley & Sons, Inc.

New York • Chichester • Weinheim • Brisbane • Singapore • Toronto

Published by John Wiley & Sons, Inc.
Published simultaneously in Canada.

No part of this publication may be reproduced, stored in a retrieval system or transmitted in any form or by any means, electronic, mechanical, photocopying, recording, scanning or otherwise, except as permitted under Sections 107 or 108 of the 1976 United States Copyright Act, without either the prior written permission of the Publisher, or authorization through payment of the appropriate per-copy fee to the Copyright Clearance Center, 222 Rosewood Drive, Danvers, MA 01923, (978) 750-8400, fax (978) 750-4744. Requests to the Publisher for permission should be addressed to the Permissions Department, John Wiley & Sons, Inc., 605 Third Avenue, New York, NY 10158-0012, (212) 850-6011, fax (212) 850-6008, e-mail: PERMREQ@WILEY.COM.

This publication is designed to provide accurate and authoritative information in regard to the subject matter covered. It is sold with the understanding that the publisher is not engaged in rendering professional services. If professional advice or other expert assistance is required, the services of a competent professional person should be sought.

Library of Congress Cataloging-in-Publication Data

Janda, Louis H.
    The psychologist's book of personality tests : twenty-four revealing tests to identify and overcome your personal barriers to a better life / Louis Janda.
        p. cm.
    ISBN 0-471-37102-5
        1. Personality tests.   I. Title.

BF698.5 J35 2001
155.2'8—dc21   00-043397

Printed in the United States of America

10 9 8 7 6 5 4 3 2 1

Contents

Section III: In Search of Self-Growth

The Psychologist's Book
of Personality Tests

Introduction

We psychologists tend to be a negative lot. We spend more of our time focusing on what is wrong with people than on what is right with them. And I think there is a good reason for this. As this is being written, near the end of 1999, the surgeon general issued a report that 22 percent of us can expect to experience a psychological disorder (some impairment in one's ability to function) during any given year and that 50 percent of us can expect to experience such a disorder at some time during our life. By definition, psychological disorders have a profound effect. They make it difficult, sometimes impossible, to get through our day-to-day routines. They can eat away at the foundation of our relationships with family, friends, and colleagues. And even if those who are suffering from a disorder manage to put on a good enough front to fool others, they do so while experiencing nearly unbearable levels of anxiety, depression, or loneliness.

For mental health professionals perhaps the most distressing element of the surgeon general's report was that a substantial majority of those who do experience a mental disorder never receive treatment for it, despite the fact that effective treatments do exist. Even though it is not necessary for them to suffer alone, millions of people live with their painful emotions, struggling to make it through each day. It is for people such as these, perhaps people like you, that I wrote this book. My hope is that this book will help you to begin the process of recognizing and overcoming your barriers to having a more satisfying and effective life.

Because we psychologists do focus more on what is wrong with our clients than on what is right, we have not come close to reaching a consensus as to how to define a fully functioning, highly adjusted individual. But we have reached a high degree of consensus about the problems that prevent people from reaching this state. We mental health professionals have a rich vocabulary filled with impressive-sounding scientific jargon to label these problems, but I like to think of them as barriers—barriers that make it difficult for people to get all they can from their life. The tests in the first two sections of this book can help you to identify your barriers and provide you with some ideas as to how you can get started on the task of removing these obstacles so that you can live a more satisfying, effective life.

The tests in the first section, Personal Barriers, measure qualities that have an impact on our moods and emotions. The Self-Esteem Rating Scale represents what many would view as the cornerstone of adjustment; it is nearly impossible to function effectively and happily if we have a poor view of ourselves. As the title of the test in chapter 2 suggests, the Four Systems Anxiety Questionnaire measures the degree of anxiety and stress we experience. Not only is it nearly impossible to enjoy life if we are chronically anxious, but these feelings will also almost guarantee that we will not function at full capacity. The Automatic Thoughts Questionnaire in chapter 3 measures what has been called the common cold of psychopathology—depression. This test reflects a current theory suggesting that our thoughts, or cognitions as we psychologists like to call them, play a major role in our moods. It simply is not necessary to feel this way so much of the time. The Personal Behavior Inventory, found in chapter 4, measures the subtle but crucial beliefs we have about the forces that control our behavior. People who feel relatively helpless about changing their lot in life tend to create self-fulfilling prophecies. The Survey of Personal Beliefs, presented in chapter 5, measures beliefs that distort our view of ourselves and the world. To have effective, satisfying lives, we must see the world as it really is. If we are to accomplish our goals and get everything from life that we want, we have to be able to make some sacrifices in the short term. The Barratt Impulsiveness Scale, found in chapter 6, can help you learn if you have this important quality. One barrier that many people would never consider unless they have experienced it themselves concerns our body image—our feelings about our physical appearance. The Multidimensional Body-Self Relations Questionnaire in chapter 7 measures these feelings, which can profoundly affect the way we view and feel about ourselves. Finally, the "Why Worry" Scale in chapter 8 measures the degree to which our chronic, and often unnecessary, worries affect our day-to-day functioning.

The tests in section II measure barriers that interfere with our interpersonal relationships. Fully functioning and happy people are able to connect with others and be straightforward and honest in their relationships with not only friends and loved ones but with strangers and acquaintances as well. The Friendliness Scale is presented in chapter 9. The old cliché "to have a friend, you must be a friend" does have scientific support. The Adult Self-Expression Scale, presented in chapter 10, measures assertiveness and the ability to express one's feelings in a socially acceptable way—a skill that is crucial to establishing satisfying and effective relationships. The Fear of Intimacy Scale, found in chapter 11, measures barriers to achieving a real and meaningful connection with others. The Way of Life Scale, found in chapter 12, was developed to measure the Type A personality. This term is usually associated with sufferers of coronary heart disease, but as you will see, it also has important implications for close relationships with others. The title of the test in chapter 13, the Multidimensional Anger Inventory, says it all. Although angry people may not recognize that their feelings are a barrier to forming effective relationships, their outbursts of temper are likely to drive others away. Our ability to trust those we have close relationships with is critical to how satisfied we are with them, and this is measured by the Specific Interpersonal Trust Scale, found in chapter

14. Perhaps nothing can add to the satisfaction we feel when we have a happy, successful romantic relationship, and the test in chapter 15, the Romantic Relationship Scale, can provide you with an idea if your barriers are getting in the way. Finally, in chapter 16, the Revised Mosher Guilt Inventory can help you learn if you have barriers that are interfering with your sexual relationships, this most pleasurable form of human interaction.

The tests in section III, In Search of Self-Growth, have a different focus: they reflect the work of psychologists who have asked what makes happy, effective people different from those with problems. These tests will provide you with an index of your strengths, the qualities you have that will enable you to reach your full potential. The Negative Mood Regulation Scale, found in chapter 17, measures the ability to take action to get past distressing feelings, an ability that anyone can develop with practice and persistence. The Self-Efficacy Scale, presented in chapter 18, measures the qualities of people who have a "can-do" attitude. These people believe they can overcome the barriers that stand in the way of their getting what they want. The Hardiness Scale, found in chapter 19, was originally intended to measure the capacity to deal with stress, but it may provide a good index of your overall mental health. The Thriving Scale, presented in chapter 20, measures one's ability to find something positive and to experience personal growth when faced with adversity. The Empathy Scale, presented in chapter 21, measures a quality that I believe is essential to a civilized, humane society—the ability to identify with the emotional experiences of others. The final three tests, although developed using rigorous scientific methods, reflect more theoretical notions about what it means to be a highly functioning, mentally healthy person. The Sense of Symbolic Immortality Scale, found in chapter 22, reflects the belief of many psychologists that it is necessary to come to terms with our limited time on earth if we are to find meaning in our lives. I included the Neophilia Scale in chapter 23 because I believe that an appreciation and desire for new experiences is critical to the ability to find life both interesting and challenging. The final test in the book, in chapter 24, is the Peak Experiences Scale. It measures the ability to experience those rare moments of pure joy that are thought to be characteristic of the most highly functioning people. I hope everyone who takes advantage of the information in this book will have many such moments.

A Few Words about Self-Report Tests

All of the tests in this book are called self-report tests because they rely on information that you are willing to provide. Such tests are useful to psychologists because they provide an idea of how any one person compares to others. But because they are self-report tests, you are unlikely to learn anything about yourself that you didn't already know. So, for example, if you receive a high score on the Automatic Thoughts Questionnaire, you already knew you were depressed; it did not take this test to make you aware of this. The goal of this book is not to provide you with startling new information about yourself, but rather to help you articulate and achieve a better understanding of the barriers that are standing in your way of a more satisfying and effective life. Also, it is important to appreciate that all of the tests in this book were developed by research psychologists to aid in understanding the various barriers, or problems, presented here. In almost all the cases, the norms were based on college students and not clinical patients. This means that no matter how high, or low, you score on any of the tests in this book, it would not be correct to conclude that you are mentally ill. Yes, it may be true that you have a diagnosable condition, but the only way you can know for certain is by consulting a mental health professional. This book simply cannot provide, nor is it intended to provide, enough information for you to come to this conclusion.

As you work your way through the book, you will notice that some of the items on the various tests are not directly relevant to your situation. You will be asked about disciplining your children, your relationship with your family, or your feelings about colleagues at work, situations that not everyone has experienced. When you come across one of these items that does not apply to your life, try to answer it as you imagine you would feel if you had such an experience. Even though your response is only your best guess, by responding to such items your final score will be more accurate than it would be had you skipped over the item.

Please use the book as I have intended. Use it as a guide for organizing your thoughts about your life and the barriers that are preventing you from getting what you want out of life and your relationships. Use it as a starting place for making the changes that will help you accomplish your goals. You can even use it with your spouse or a close friend to help you better understand any conflicts you may be having in your relationships. We do not always see ourselves as others do. But remember, this book is only a place for you to begin to ask the relevant questions and to begin your search for the appropriate answers. I hope you enjoy the process of self-discovery and find it as useful as I wish it to be for you.

A Few Words about Scoring

After each test you will find directions for scoring your responses to the items. The instructions are straightforward, but there is one concept that can be a little confusing for those who encounter it for the first time—namely "reverse scoring." To illustrate, you might be taking a test to measure your level of extroversion and the instructions require you to respond using a scale of 1 to 5, where 1 indicated "not at all," 2 indicated "sometimes," 3 indicated "moderately often," 4 indicated "often," and 5 indicated "all the time." Now imagine the following two items:

1. I like wild parties.
2. I like to stay home and read on Saturday nights.

If you are an extreme extrovert, you would most likely respond with a 5 to the first item and a 1 to the second item. If we want high scores on the test to indicate high levels of extroversion, we would have to "reverse score" the second item. This means that a response of 5 would be changed to a 1, a 4 would be changed to a 2, a 3 would remain a 3, a 2 would be changed to a 4, and a 1 would be changed to a 5. So, after we reverse score the second item, you would receive the maximum score of 10. In the instructions for scoring that follow each test, the items that require reverse scoring will be indicated.

A Few Words about Norms

Norms are a tool used by psychologists to give raw test scores meaning. To illustrate the point, suppose that after taking the SAT or some other college entrance exam, you were told that you answered 55 questions correctly. You would have no idea if this was a good score or if it meant you should rethink your plans for college. To help you understand your performance, the test publisher transforms the number of questions you answered correctly into a normative score. With the SAT, as most of you know, your score would fall somewhere between 200 and 800. This is one form of a normative score, and it makes it possible for you to know how you performed relative to other people.

One of the most basic types of normative scores, and the one I use in this book, is called a percentile. Percentiles indicate the rank of your score compared to other people. I use five percentile ranks for each of the tests in this book: 85, 70, 50, 30, and 15. A percentile score of 85 means that your score was higher than 85 percent of the people in the normative sample who took the test, a percentile score of 70 means that your score was higher than 70 percent of the people, and so on. These five points will give you a good idea of how you stand relative to others.

One last concept and then the statistics lesson is over. In the process of developing a test, psychologists give it to a group of people in order to establish the norms. This group of people is called the normative sample, and it is important to know something about the sample to understand what your test score means. For instance, scoring at the 85th percentile on a test of anxiety would mean something quite different if the normative sample consisted of typical college students rather than hospitalized psychiatric patients. In the first case, you are at the high end of the normal population. In the second case, your anxiety level would represent a much more serious problem.

It is very important that you keep in mind that all of the norms presented in this book were based on typical people. In most cases, the normative sample consisted of college students, and for the other tests, the normative sample consisted of typical adults without any known psychological disorders. So, even if you received a score well above the 85th percentile on a test, it does not necessarily mean that you have a psychological disorder. It simply means that, in the case of an anxiety test, you have an above average level of anxiety. You are the best judge of how serious your problem is, and though taking a test will help you to clarify your thoughts about your situation, it will not provide a substitute for your own good sense about your situation. Use these tests as a guide for change, not as the final word about your state of mind.

Time to Get Started

Keeping all this in mind, you are ready to begin with the tests. I have arranged them in an order that makes sense to me, but feel free to take them in any order you like. You may even want to begin with the tests in section III to learn about your strengths before you tackle your barriers. But most of all, I hope you can enjoy the process of self-discovery and find information in this book that will help you have a more satisfying and effective life. Good luck!

SECTION I

PERSONAL BARRIERS

1
How Do You Feel about Yourself?

THE SELF-ESTEEM
RATING SCALE

This questionnaire is designed to measure how you feel about yourself. It is not a test, so there are no right or wrong answers. Please answer each item as carefully and accurately as you can by placing a number by each one as follows:

1 = Never
2 = Rarely
3 = A little of the time
4 = Some of the time
5 = A good part of the time
6 = Most of the time
7 = Always

_____ 1. I feel that people would *not* like me if they really knew me well.

_____ 2. I feel that others do things much better than I do.

_____ 3. I feel that I am an attractive person.

_____ 4. I feel confident in my ability to deal with other people.

_____ 5. I feel that I am likely to fail at things I do.

_____ 6. I feel that people really like to talk with me.

_____ 7. I feel that I am a very competent person.

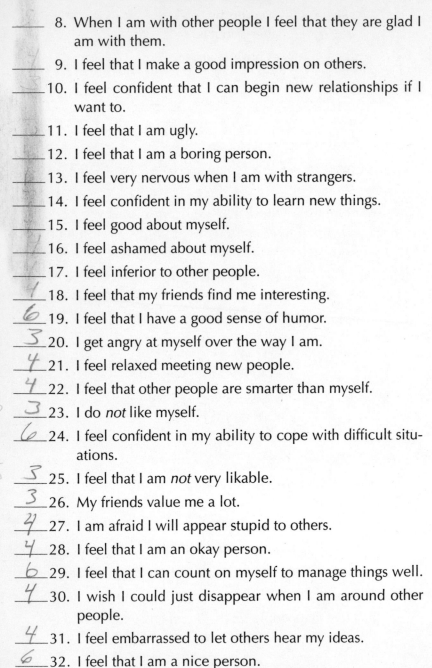

_____ 8. When I am with other people I feel that they are glad I am with them.

_____ 9. I feel that I make a good impression on others.

_____ 10. I feel confident that I can begin new relationships if I want to.

_____ 11. I feel that I am ugly.

_____ 12. I feel that I am a boring person.

_____ 13. I feel very nervous when I am with strangers.

_____ 14. I feel confident in my ability to learn new things.

_____ 15. I feel good about myself.

_____ 16. I feel ashamed about myself.

_____ 17. I feel inferior to other people.

_____ 18. I feel that my friends find me interesting.

_6_ 19. I feel that I have a good sense of humor.

_3_ 20. I get angry at myself over the way I am.

_4_ 21. I feel relaxed meeting new people.

_4_ 22. I feel that other people are smarter than myself.

_3_ 23. I do *not* like myself.

_6_ 24. I feel confident in my ability to cope with difficult situations.

_3_ 25. I feel that I am *not* very likable.

_3_ 26. My friends value me a lot.

_4_ 27. I am afraid I will appear stupid to others.

_4_ 28. I feel that I am an okay person.

_6_ 29. I feel that I can count on myself to manage things well.

_4_ 30. I wish I could just disappear when I am around other people.

_4_ 31. I feel embarrassed to let others hear my ideas.

_6_ 32. I feel that I am a nice person.

_4__ 33. I feel that if I could be more like other people then I would feel better about myself.

_5__ 34. I feel that I get pushed around more than others.

_4__ 35. I feel that people like me.

____ 36. I feel that people have a good time when they are with me.

_6__ 37. I feel confident that I can do well in whatever I do.

_5__ 38. I trust the competence of others more than I trust my own abilities.

_4__ 39. I feel that I mess things up.

_2__ 40. I wish that I were someone else.

Reprinted with permission of Dr. William R. Nugent. For more information see: W. R. Nugent, and J. W. Thomas (1993). "Validation of the Self-Esteem Rating Scale," *Research on Social Work Practice* 3, 191–207.

SCORING

The following items must be reversed (1 = 7, 2 = 6, 3 = 5, 4 = 4, 5 = 3, 6 = 2, and 7 = 1): 1, 2, 5, 11, 13, 16, 17, 20, 22, 23, 25, 27, 30, 31, 33, 34, 38, 39, and 40. After reversing these items, add your responses together to obtain your final score.

NORMS

Score	Percentile
260	85
244	70
227	50
210	30
194	15

About the Self-Esteem Rating Scale

Over the past decade or so, there has been an interesting turn-about regarding how people view self-esteem. Twenty years ago, the evidence seemed clear that high self-esteem was crucial if people were to have happy, productive lives. Nowhere was this belief more influential than in the school system. Research conducted in the 1960s appeared to prove that school achievement was influenced more by children's self-esteem than by their intellectual ability. These studies inspired educators to do everything they could to help children feel better about themselves in the belief that this would help them become better students. As everyone knows, these programs have become the target of numerous vitriolic critics.

Research in psychology is always difficult. A typical study may focus on a handful of variables while, because of practical limitations, it ignores countless other variables that are potentially important. This means that virtually any research study is open to alternative interpretations, and it is up to subsequent researchers to untangle the myriad possibilities that account for the results of any one study. I believe this is what happened to the research regarding the relationship between self-esteem and school achievement in the 1960s. People were too quick to accept the results at face value. Before designing school programs that focused on increasing children's self-esteem, they would have been well advised to wait for further research to provide a clearer picture as to how things really worked.

Had they waited a few years, the educational gurus who wanted "I am a wonderful person" to be every child's mantra would have realized that high self-esteem in a vacuum is not necessarily a good thing. Children who are praised for their ability regardless of their work are likely to learn that not much is expected of them; they would have every reason to feel good about themselves even if they produce mediocre results. We know that children are more likely to master difficult material if we comment on their efforts rather than on their ability. Indeed, psychologist Carol Dweck found that the performance of students who were given tasks that were too difficult to complete and were told that they failed because they did not try hard enough improved more than students who were given easy tasks in order to encourage them to feel good about their ability. The moral of the story is clear—self-esteem should be earned, not provided unconditionally.

Indeed, extremely high self-esteem may be a sign of maladjustment. We have all known people who think they are the most wonderful human beings alive, even though their flaws and limitations are obvious to all who care to take even a cursory look. Sometimes called defensive high self-esteem, the people with this quality seem to be capable of putting a positive spin on even the worst failures. It appears to be the case that people with moderately high self-esteem are the best adjusted. They generally feel good about themselves, but they are capable of acknowledging their flaws and doing something about them.

Now that I've vented my frustrations about the view that all children should be praised unconditionally, let me say that I have seen a number of clients who suffered terribly from poor self-esteem. Perhaps one of the most poignant examples was a graduate student I'll call Doug. He suffered from intense anxiety and depression even though his life was going pretty well. Doug had had a successful academic career, was married to a woman who loved him, and was a doting, caring father. Yet he was incapable of articulating anything good about himself. During one therapy session, I told him I was going no further until he could say one positive thing about himself. He spent five agitated minutes mulling over possibilities before he said, "I *used* to play the piano well." When I told him that he had to tell me something good about himself in the present, he was completely stumped. I finally gave in and asked him to tell me what his wife would say about his good qualities. He was able to list several qualities she would point to, but then immediately dismissed them as unreliable. After all, Doug's wife loved him and consequently she could not be objective. Just as people with defensive high self-esteem cannot acknowledge any negative information about themselves, people such as Doug cannot recognize anything positive about themselves.

If you scored below the 30th percentile on the Self-Esteem Rating Scale, you undoubtedly deserve to feel better about yourself. I do not believe that people should have unequivocally positive feelings about themselves, but I do believe that almost everyone deserves to feel generally good about the kind of person they are. The first piece of evidence that you deserve to feel better about yourself is that you are reading these words. That means that you care about becoming a better person, and you care about how others react to you. And people with modest self-esteem often make caring, loyal friends. Because they are convinced of their own inadequacies, they are more than happy to shift the focus of attention away from themselves onto those around them. Unless your poor self-esteem has caused you to cut yourself off from others completely, you probably have several people in your life who care about you and value the time they spend with you. That alone shows you have reason to feel good about yourself.

A second key to feeling better about yourself is to accept that you do not have to be perfect in order to feel good about yourself. Poor self-esteem was one of my struggles when I was younger, and this was a lesson I learned only over time. No, I had to admit, I was not brilliant, but I came to accept that I was smart enough to get a Ph.D. and to do my job reasonably well. No, I was not a Robert Redford clone, but I was presentable enough to entice an attractive, vivacious woman to marry me. And no, I was not the most outgoing, entertaining guy around, but I was interesting enough to develop a valued circle of friends.

It took me many years before I felt generally comfortable with myself, but you can speed up the process by making a concerted effort. Make a list of your strengths. Ask your family and friends for their suggestions. When you find yourself obsessing about your limitations, get out your list and read it out loud. You can also use your self-doubts to your advantage. If you are convinced your negative self-evaluation is justified, do something about it. I have known students who have a low opinion of their academic abilities who use their feelings as an excuse for giving up. They skip class, fail to prepare for tests, and then complain, "See, I just can't hack it." Your self-doubts should motivate you to do your best. And if your best is still not good enough, you can be sure that there is something else you can do where your best will be more than good enough. As long as you do not give up, you can feel good about yourself. It's up to you.

2

How Anxious Are You?

THE FOUR SYSTEMS ANXIETY QUESTIONNAIRE

This questionnaire contains sixty items concerning difficulties that most people experience from time to time. Read each item carefully. If you have experienced any of the thoughts, feelings, physical symptoms, or behaviors in the manner indicated by any of the items, respond with "Yes." If you have not, respond with a "No." Please make sure that none of the items are omitted. Please do not spend too much time on any question. We are interested in your first reaction, not a deeply considered response.

_no_ _4_ 1. I blush easily.

_no_ _4_ 2. I often feel so helpless and desperate that life becomes a source of suffering for me.

yes _5_ 3. Poor sleep is one of my biggest problems.

yes _6_ 4. I often avoid talking to people in a train or on a bus.

yes _6_ 5. I tend to avoid going out.

_no_ _2_ 6. I often have a headache.

_no_ _4_ 7. I often experience the feeling of embarrassment.

yes _5_ 8. A jittery feeling has become part of my life.

yes _5_ 9. I often have dizzy attacks.

yes _5_ 10. I sometimes cannot think of anything except for my worries.

no   *1*   11. I seldom experience chest pain.

yes   *5*   12. I seldom feel on edge.

yes   *4*   13. I cannot concentrate on a task because of disruption by uncontrolled thoughts.

yes   *6*   14. I rarely feel joyful.

yes   *6*   15. I have persistent disturbing thoughts.

yes   *6*   16. I definitely avoid going to any kind of place again where I previously had a difficult time (for example, a social gathering or a street, etc.).

yes   *5*   17. I sometimes think of myself as an inefficient person.

yes   *4*   18. My feelings dominate my personality so much that I have no control over them.

yes   *5*   19. I worry a lot when I think of possible disapproval from others.

no   *3*   20. I often experience the feeling of excitement.

no   *2*   21. I rarely try to steer clear of challenging jobs.

no   *2*   22. I rarely have disturbed sleep.

yes   *6*   23. I sometimes feel upset.

yes   *5*   24. My muscles are quite tense throughout the day.

no   *4*   25. When at home I usually try not to stay alone at night.

yes   *5*   26. I sometimes get easily tired even when not working hard.

no   *3*   27. I rarely worry about unimportant events.

no   *2*   28. I seldom laugh freely.

no   *2*   29. I usually worry that I will not be able to cope with difficulties in my life.

yes   *5*   30. I tend to avoid talking to someone who is above me such as my boss.

no   *3*   31. I rarely find myself lost in worrying.

yes _3_ 32. Wherever I go or whatever I do, I always have a feeling of discomfort.

yes _4_ 33. I sometimes avoid participating in discussions even though I know the topic well.

no _2_ 34. My hands rarely shake.

yes _5_ 35. I sometimes feel extremely self-conscious.

yes _6_ 36. I am worried that others might misunderstand me.

no _1_ 37. I occasionally experience a tingling sensation around my body.

no _3_ 38. I rarely try to keep away from social gatherings.

yes _5_ 39. I sometimes feel happy but it easily fades away.

yes _6_ 40. Even if everything is going well, my mind is occupied by imagining upsetting ideas.

yes _7_ 41. I seldom have palpitations.

yes _5_ 42. I cannot think clearly about anything because disrupting thoughts keep occurring in my mind.

no _1_ 43. There seems to be a lump in my throat much of the time.

yes _4_ 44. I cannot feel relaxed even though I am not in a hurry.

no _3_ 45. I seldom avoid speaking at social occasions.

no _2_ 46. Even if it is necessary, I sometimes avoid asking other people questions.

no _2_ 47. I very rarely imagine myself being unpopular with my friends.

yes _4_ 48. I have diarrhea once a month or more.

yes _6_ 49. I often find myself thinking about possible embarrassing situations.

yes _4_ 50. I usually feel quite insecure in my life.

yes _5_ 51. I have a tight sensation at my neck.

yes _4_ 52. I usually avoid getting involved in social activity.

yes _6_ 53. My uneasy feelings flare up at any moment.

no _5_ 54. I usually try to avoid walking in crowded streets.

yes _5_ 55. I always feel irritable.

yes _6_ 56. I hardly ever tell jokes.

yes _4_ 57. I am concerned about how others view me.

no _2_ 58. I sometimes have stomach problems.

yes _5_ 59. Half of my thoughts are related to some kinds of worries.

yes _2_ 60. I try to avoid standing up to other people even if they have taken advantage of me.

Reprinted with the permission of Dr. Falih Koksal of the University of Stirling in Scotland. For more information see: F. Koksal, and D. G. Power (1990). "Four Systems Anxiety Questionnaire (FSAQ): A Self-Report Measure of Somatic, Cognitive, Behavioral, and Feeling Components." *Journal of Personality Assessment*, 54, 534–45.

SCORING

A different method of test construction was used to develop the Four Systems Anxiety Questionnaire than the other tests in this book and consequently the scoring system is quite different. Each item has a scale value, and to find your score on the four subscales and your total score you must add together values for each item that you responded to with a "Yes." The values for each item and the subscale it belongs to are provided below. To find your total score, simply add your four subscale scores together.

Feeling		Cognitive		Behavioral		Somatic	
2.	8.6	10.	8.1	4.	3.6	1.	6.6
7.	4.4	13.	8.5	5.	9.0	3.	7.9
8.	7.8	15.	7.8	16.	7.4	6.	6.7
12.	1.0	17.	4.5	21.	1.1	9.	8.5
14.	2.8	19.	6.4	25.	7.0	11.	1.4
18.	8.2	27.	1.0	28.	6.8	22.	1.3
20.	3.1	29.	7.0	30.	6.4	24.	8.2
23.	1.9	31.	1.1	33.	6.0	26.	5.7
32.	7.9	36.	4.7	38.	1.1	34.	1.4
35.	5.2	40.	8.1	45.	1.1	37.	4.8
39.	3.7	42.	8.5	46.	6.8	41.	1.5
44.	6.9	47.	1.0	52.	7.7	43.	8.2
50.	6.1	49.	5.9	54.	7.5	48.	6.7
53.	7.5	57.	3.1	56.	4.6	51.	7.2
55.	7.3	59.	6.7	60.	6.4	58.	6.3

NORMS

SCORES					PERCENTILE
Feeling	Cognitive	Behavioral	Somatic	Total	
31	42	33	31	128	85
24	33	27	25	105	70
17	24	20	19	81	50
10	15	13	13	57	30
3	6	7	7	34	15

52.3 72.3 51.1 45.7 221.4

About the Four Systems Anxiety Questionnaire

Psychologists have known for several decades that anxiety is a multifaceted concept. While all of us would acknowledge having experienced anxiety, the reality is that our experience of "feeling anxious" is probably quite different from how others experience this emotion. Nearly thirty years ago, psychologist Peter Lang proposed three ways in which anxiety can be experienced. The first can be called the cognitive component—what people say to themselves or what they report to others. A man with a dog phobia, for instance, might say "I'm terrified" when he sees a Rotweiller running toward him. The second component is the physiological or somatic reaction. In our example, the dog-phobic man may experience a pounding heart or a knot in his stomach when he spots the Rotweiller. The third component of anxiety is behavioral—what our man does when he spots the dog. If he turns to run away, we can be safe in concluding that he is exhibiting a behavioral sign of anxiety.

What makes this concept so interesting is that these three components of anxiety do not correspond with one another very well. In our example above, this man may report to others that he is terrified of dogs, but he may not experience very much physiological arousal when he sees one. As a second example, I know a couple where the wife reports having a mild fear of public speaking, but despite her claim that her fear is slight, she absolutely refuses all invitations to talk to a group, even though it would be good for her business. Her husband, on the other hand, reports a pounding heart and feelings of sheer terror while speaking to groups, but he forces himself to accept invitations nonetheless. We cannot use what people say about themselves to predict with any accuracy what is going on inside them or how they will behave.

Falih Koksal and Kevin Power took this conceptualization of anxiety one step further. They argued that the cognitive component of anxiety can be divided further—to the types of verbal self-statements people make and the subjective feelings they report. Verbal self-statements would be represented by item 10, "I sometimes cannot think of anything except for my worries," while subjective feelings are typified by item 7, "I often experience the feeling of embarrassment." They found enough evidence to support the four distinct dimensions of their Four Systems Anxiety Questionnaire, although they did report that verbal self-statements and subjective feelings were highly interrelated. As did previous researchers, they found much less overlap between these two components of cognitive anxiety and either somatic or behavioral anxiety.

Your scores on the Four Systems Anxiety Questionnaire will enable you to better understand how you experience anxiety. This is important, because the way in which you experience this emotion has important implications as to what you can do about it. If your highest score was on either the Feeling or Cognitive subscales, then modifying your cognitions is likely to be especially helpful. We will discuss this approach in detail in chapter 3, which deals with depression and the Automatic Thoughts Questionnaire, where the same principles apply. Using the test items as a guide, identify your irrational cognitions and write out more adaptive, rational thoughts you can use instead.

If your highest score was on the Somatic subscale, relaxation techniques can be especially effective. Psychologist Arnold Lazarus has published audiotapes that can guide you through these exercises. Remember, it takes some time to change your body's response to anxiety-provoking situations, so be patient, but practice both regularly and diligently.

Let us spend more time focusing on behavioral anxiety. If your highest score was on this scale, you are the sort of person who avoids situations because you anticipate they will make you feel anxious. People who allow their anxiety to influence their behavior tend to have restricted lives, which in turn can lead to depression. As always, if your tendency to avoid situations is severe, you should consult a mental health professional. It simply is not necessary for you to suffer so. But if you have a milder case of behavioral anxiety, you may be able to treat yourself successfully using a technique called in vivo desensitization. This term describes a process of overcoming anxiety by exposing oneself gradually to the real-life situations that elicit the anxiety. I met a woman once who successfully treated herself for agoraphobia using this technique even though she had never heard about it before. It is a commonsense approach that can be quite effective.

This woman, I'll call her Susan, developed a fear of leaving her house shortly after the birth of her first child. Within a few months, her fear was so severe that she would not venture past her front door unless she was accompanied by her husband. After suffering from this debilitating anxiety for several more months, she decided she had to do something about it. Intuitively, she concluded that the best way to overcome her fear was to attack it in small steps. So, for the first week, her goal was simply to walk out the front door and stand on her porch for brief periods of time. The first day, she was able to do this for less than a minute, but by the end of the week, she could stand outdoors for ten minutes without feeling uncomfortable. Her next goal was to walk down to the curb to check her mailbox. This took her nearly two weeks. At first, she would take a few steps off the porch and would feel overwhelmed by the anxiety. But each day she forced herself to take an additional step, and by the end of the second week, she could stand by the mailbox and look through her mail without any sense of panic.

Each time Susan accomplished one goal, she would set a slightly more ambitious goal for her next step. Her progress was slow but steady, and by the end of a year Susan was able to go where she wanted by herself. For several more months, she always felt "on edge" during these excursions, and occasionally the anxiety would become quite intense. During these episodes, she would park her car or sit on a bench until she could feel herself relax.

Others who have experienced agoraphobia may marvel at Susan's willpower, but behavior therapists who teach this technique would argue that it was Susan's "skill power," not her willpower, that allowed her to overcome her fear. Although she had no knowledge of behavioral psychology, Susan was able to skillfully apply these techniques to deal with her situation. The key was that she was persistent and that she did not give up.

3
How Depressed Are You?

> ## THE AUTOMATIC
> ## THOUGHTS QUESTIONNAIRE

Listed below are a variety of thoughts that pop into people's heads. Please read each thought and indicate how frequently, if at all, the thought occurred to you *over the last week*. Please read each item carefully and indicate the appropriate response, using the scale below.

> 5 = All the time
> 4 = Often
> 3 = Moderately often
> 2 = Sometimes
> 1 = Not at all

_____ 1. I feel like I'm up against the world.

_____ 2. I'm no good.

_____ 3. Why can't I ever succeed?

_____ 4. No one understands me.

_____ 5. I've let people down.

_____ 6. I don't think I can go on.

_____ 7. I wish I were a better person.

_____ 8. I'm so weak.

_____ 9. My life's not going the way I want it to.

_3_ 10. I'm so disappointed in myself.

_4_ 11. Nothing feels good anymore.

_4_ 12. I can't stand this anymore.

_4_ 13. I can't get started.

_4_ 14. What's wrong with me?

_2_ 15. I wish I were somewhere else.

_4_ 16. I can't get things together.

_4_ 17. I hate myself.

_4_ 18. I'm worthless.

_4_ 19. I wish I could just disappear.

_4_ 20. What's the matter with me?

_4_ 21. I'm a loser.

_4_ 22. My life is a mess.

_4_ 23. I'm a failure.

_4_ 24. I'll never make it.

_4_ 25. I feel so helpless.

_4_ 26. Something has to change.

_4_ 27. There must be something wrong with me.

_4_ 28. My future is bleak.

_3_ 29. It's just not worth it.

_4_ 30. I can't finish anything.

Reprinted with permission of Dr. Steven D. Hollon of Vanderbilt University. For more information see: S. D. Hollon, and P. C. Kendall (1980). "Cognitive Self-Statements in Depression: Development of an Automatic Thoughts Questionnaire." *Cognitive Therapy and Research,* 4, 383–95.

SCORING

To find your score, simply add together your responses for the 30 items.

NORMS

SCORE	PERCENTILE
60	85
55	70
49	50
43	30
38	15

About the Automatic Thoughts Questionnaire

We have learned a great deal about depression over the past few decades. Much of this research has focused on the biological underpinnings of depression, and this work has led to a number of new and effective medications. And while these advances have undoubtedly helped to improve the quality of life for countless people, a number of people, including yours truly, are concerned that the biological view of depression has been oversold. We are living in a time when Prozac is one of the medications most widely prescribed not only by psychiatrists but by family practitioners as well. Although it seems like a simple solution to life's problems, there is good reason to believe that taking a pill is not always the best solution for depression.

Among those with a healthy dose of skepticism about drugs always being the best answer are the authors of the Automatic Thoughts Questionnaire, Drs. Steven Hollon and Philip Kendall.

They argue that thoughts play a critical role. A number of investigators have collected convincing evidence that certain thoughts, or cognitions, can both initiate and maintain a depressive episode. Hollon and Kendall developed the Automatic Thoughts Questionnaire to assess the sorts of cognitions that are associated with depression. Their goal was to develop a test that would be useful in gauging the progress of psychotherapy, but it can also be useful for those of you who are prone to experiencing these feelings. If you do have such episodes and you had a high score on this test, the odds are excellent that by changing your automatic thoughts you could feel considerably better. Please note that the norms were based on nondepressed college students. So even if your score was above the 85th percentile, it does not necessarily mean that you are seriously depressed. As always, if you suspect that you are, you should consult a mental health professional.

I know all too well that changing one's thoughts is easier said than done, but it can be accomplished with a concerted effort. The first step is to recognize that the types of thoughts reflected in the items in this test are indeed irrational—but recognizing this is often difficult for depressed people to do. I had a client a few years ago, for instance, who came to therapy for help with her depression. This young woman was about to graduate from a prestigious university and had been accepted to an equally prestigious graduate school where she planned to obtain her Ph.D. Sounds impressive, right? Well, she was depressed because she was "such a failure." As evidence, she pointed to her rejection from her first choice of a graduate school and to two classmates who had higher grade point averages than her own.

What seems so obvious to an outside observer can be impossible for the depressed person to believe. I'm not sure I ever completely convinced this young woman that her assessment of herself as a failure was irrational. She was saying the right things by the end of our brief therapy and she reported feeling better, but I suspect that she continued to harbor the belief that she was a failure because she did not graduate number one in her class and was not accepted to the most prestigious graduate school.

The truth is that the sorts of thoughts people have can be, and often are, independent of what they are doing with their lives. We have all known people who seem to make a mess of everything they try, yet they remain convinced that their only problem is that others fail to recognize their greatness. The important point is that even when we experience disappointments, we are not justified in concluding that we are worthless or doomed to a life of failure.

The first step in modifying the automatic thoughts that are contributing to your feelings of depression is to go through the list of items and find a more realistic view for those that you endorsed. Most depressed people, for instance, endorse item 21, "I'm a loser." They may even cite a failure or two as examples of what losers they are. But we've all heard stories of people who have had countless failures before they reached their goals. Having a failure experience is just that—a failure experience. It does not make one a loser.

The next step is to make a concerted effort to substitute a more realistic, positive thought every time you experience the negative thought. If you have the persistent thought, for instance, that you are a loser, have a substitute thought ready. Perhaps it would be, "Yes, I failed at that project, but the next time around I'll be ready and I'll do better." Another good thought would be, "Yes, I failed at that project, but let me review all the successes that I've had." Thoughts can be habits the same way that behaviors are. So just as one can conquer the bad habit of biting one's fingernails by engaging in a substitute behavior whenever the urge to bite strikes, one can modify negative automatic thoughts with a sustained effort to substitute more positive, realistic thoughts for the negative automatic thoughts.

This approach to treating depression is called cognitive therapy. Aaron Beck is responsible for articulating this theory, and he has suggested that depressed people tend to make several types of logical errors in their thinking. Magnification and minimization are two common such errors—errors that my young client described above was guilty of making. She magnified her failures—namely, her "failure" to graduate at the top of her class and her failure to gain admission to her first choice of graduate school. That she was unable to take pride in her graduating third in her class and being admitted to one of the top graduate programs in the country was a result of her tendency toward minimization. Another common error described by Beck is arbitrary inference. An example of this is the person who believes that a flat tire is evidence that he or she is a loser. Depressed people often interpret impersonal events as evidence of their failures as human beings.

The belief of researchers such as Hollon, Kendall, and Beck that cognitions are crucial is supported by evidence that cognitive therapy may be as effective as medication in the treatment of depression. This debate has not been settled, but after treatment has been concluded there is good reason to believe that people who receive cognitive therapy are less likely to have a relapse than people receiving medication. I suspect the debate as to which form of treatment is best will not be resolved anytime soon, but the evidence is clear that modifying cognitions can play a very important role in alleviating depression for many people. It is hard work, but I urge you to give it a try if depression is one of your barriers to a happier, more satisfying life.

4

Who Controls Your Fate?

The following statements describe how people feel about themselves and other people. Read each statement carefully, then mark how much you agree or disagree with it, using the scale below:

> 5 = Strongly agree
> 4 = Agree
> 3 = Neither agree nor disagree
> 2 = Disagree
> 1 = Strongly disagree

___2___ 1. I live too much by other people's standards.

___2___ 2. In order to get along and be liked, I tend to be what people expect me to be rather than anything else.

___4___ 3. I guess I put on a show to impress people. I know I'm not the person I pretend to be.

___3___ 4. I change my opinion (or the way I do things) in order to please someone else.

___4___ 5. I have to be careful at parties and social gatherings for fear I will do or say things that others won't like.

_4_ 6. In class, or in a group, I am unlikely to express my opinion because I fear that others may not think well of it or of me.

_4_ 7. I keep still or tell "little white lies" in the company of my friends so as not to reveal to them that I am different (or think differently) from them.

_3_ 8. There are many aspects of my behavior over which I have very little control.

_2_ 9. I often find that my own inclinations have little to do with what I actually do or say.

_2_ 10. I have trouble taking orders because they often conflict with my own inclinations.

_4_ 11. I always practice what I preach.

_3_ 12. I am basically good at following through with my plans.

_2_ 13. I never say anything I don't mean.

_4_ 14. I have my own code of behavior and I follow it to the letter.

_4_ 15. All one's behavior should be directed toward a certain small number of definite personal goals.

_4_ 16. "Tell it like it is" is always the best policy.

_4_ 17. I can make impromptu speeches even on topics about which I have almost no information.

_4_ 18. I would probably make a good actor because I can play any role.

_3_ 19. I have very little trouble changing my behavior to suit different people and different situations.

_3_ 20. In informal discussions I often speak in favor of an unpopular position in order to cause people to think more carefully about what they are saying.

_3_ 21. I can only argue for ideas to which I am strongly committed.

_3_ 22. I think that it is very hard to predict how people are going to behave.

_3_ 23. Most behavior can't be predicted in advance.

_2_ 24. Some of the things my friends decide to do often come as a great surprise to me.

_3_ 25. Once you get to know a person well, even then his behavior will often surprise you.

_4_ 26. I usually have a pretty good idea how I'm going to behave in a particular situation.

_4_ 27. I usually know what my friends are going to do.

_3_ 28. I think that most people are very predictable.

_4_ 29. Once you get to know a person well, you can usually tell what he/she is going to do.

Reprinted with permission of Dr. Barry E. Collins. For more information see: B. E. Collins, J. C. Martin, R. D. Ashmore, and L. Ross (1973). "Some Dimensions of the Internal-External Metaphor in Theories of Personality." *Journal of Personality*, 41, 472–92.

SCORING

The first step is to reverse score (5 = 1, 4 = 2, 3 = 3, 2 = 4, and 1 = 5) the following items: 10, 21, 26, 27, 28, and 29. After reverse scoring, you can find your scores on four subscales. Other-Direction (OD) is comprised of items 1 through 10; Inner-Direction (ID) consists of items 11 through 16; Lack of Constraints on Behavior (LC) is comprised of items 17 through 21; and Predictability of Behavior (Pr) is comprised of items 22 through 29.

NORMS

		SCORES		PERCENTILE
OD	*ID*	*LC*	*Pr*	
28	24	17	26	85
25	22	15	24	70
22	20	13	21	50
19	18	11	18	30
16	16	9	16	15

About the Personal Behavior Inventory

Philosophers, poets, novelists, and of course psychologists have engaged in a lively debate about the determinants of human behavior. On the one hand, there are those who argue that people are prisoners of social forces that they cannot resist. This view suggests that we all, to varying degrees, conform to the expectations that others have for us. On the other hand, there are those who believe that every person has a unique configuration that evolves from biological predispositions and early childhood experiences. This view suggests that behavior is determined by forces that lie within each individual.

Psychologist Julian Rotter entered this fray in the 1960s when he proposed a personality dimension called internal-external locus of control. Rotter argued that people varied in terms of how they perceived the world. Those who scored at the internal end of his scale believed that they were in control, that their efforts made a difference in how their lives unfolded. Those who scored at the external end of the scale believed that luck or powerful others controlled their fate. Rotter's scale inspired thousands of research studies, and it became clear that this internal-external dimension had important implications for a variety of situations. People with an internal locus of control generally seemed to have a higher level of psychological adjustment. Because they believed their efforts made a difference, they were more active in taking steps to increase the odds that they got what they wanted from life. People with an external locus of control tended to experience more depression and anxiety and viewed the world as a frightening, hostile place.

UCLA psychologist Barry Collins and his colleagues were intrigued by this conceptualization but argued that the internal-external dimension was more complex than Rotter had suggested. Their test, the Personal Behavior Inventory, was developed to explore their ideas further. As you can see from their test and the scoring system, they concluded that there were four dimensions relevant to how we view the world, the first of which they called Other-Direction. People with high scores on this scale feel pressured to conform to the expectations of others. Their low self-esteem causes them to experience anxiety should they think about saying or doing something that might displease those around them. Consequently, they feel rather powerless to control the direction of their lives.

The second dimension is called Inner-Direction, and as the items suggest, people with high scores on this scale have an inner plan or a psychological gyroscope, to use Collins's term, which guides their behavior. These people, similar to Rotter's internals, have a clear sense of the direction they want their lives to take, and they believe they have the resources to get there.

Lack of Constraints is the third dimension. People with high scores on this scale may be characterized as being creative and free spirits. Collins and his colleagues speculated that such people may be self-actualized in that they have the flexibility to be spontaneous and to adapt to a wide variety of situations. A skeptic, however, could argue that high scorers are chameleons with little sense or little concern about what is appropriate or inappropriate. I suspect a score in the 50th to the 70th percentile range is the best place to be. It is desirable to have the flexibility to adapt to different situations, but I believe a psychological gyroscope is important as well.

Finally, the fourth dimension is Predictability of Behavior, which includes the behavior of oneself as well as the behavior of others. People with high scores on this scale have more confidence in their ability to make sense of the world. Regardless of whether they are outer- or inner-directed, they believe their lives are understandable and hence, safe. People with low scores on this scale tend to view life as more chaotic and hence, dangerous. They have difficulty feeling confidence in the consequences of their actions.

I found the Personal Behavior Inventory especially fascinating because Collins demonstrated that the four dimensions on his scale were independent. Unlike Rotter, whose test suggested that one was either internal or external, Collins found that one could have high scores on both the Inner- and Other-Direction subscales of his test. It was also the case that the Lack of Constraints and Predictability of Behavior subscales were independent of the other subscales as well. This means that one person could have any number of combination of scores on the various scales. Further research is needed before we have a clear sense of the implications of the potential profiles, but I would guess that the profile indicating the highest degree of adjustment would be a low score on the Other-Direction subscale, high scores on the Inner-Direction and Predictability of Behavior subscales, and as I indicated earlier, a moderately high score on the Lack of Constraints subscale. I suspect that such people would not be unduly influenced by the expectations of others; they would have confidence that their efforts made a difference and that the world was a safe, predictable place. They would also be sufficiently free from either external or internal constraints so that they could be spontaneous and creative when the situation was appropriate. I only wish I fit that ideal profile a little more closely.

5

How Rational Are You?

THE SURVEY OF
PERSONAL BELIEFS

People have different ideas and beliefs. We are interested in your opinion about the following statements. Using the scale below, select the number that best reflects your belief about each statement.

1 = Totally agree
2 = Mostly agree
3 = Slightly agree
4 = Slightly disagree
5 = Mostly disagree
6 = Totally disagree

5 _2_ 1. Dealing with some people can be very unpleasant, but it can never be awful or horrible.

_4_ 2. When I make a mistake, I often tell myself, "I shouldn't have done that."

_2_ 3. Absolutely, people must obey the law.

5 _2_ 4. There is nothing that I "can't stand."

_2_ 5. Being ignored, or being socially awkward at a party, would reduce my sense of self-worth.

_2_ 6. Some situations in life are truly terrible.

_5_ 7. In some areas I absolutely should be more competent.

_3_ 8. My parents should be reasonable in what they ask of me.

_2_ 9. There are some things that I just can't stand.

4 _3_ 10. My self-worth is not higher because of my successes in school or on the job.

_2_ 11. The way some children behave is just awful.

_4_ 12. I absolutely should not have made certain obvious mistakes in my life.

3 _4_ 13. Even if they had promised, and it was important to me, there is no reason why my friends have to do what I want.

_2_ 14. I can't deal with it when my friends (or my children) behave immaturely, wildly, or improperly.

_4_ 15. There are good people and bad people, as can be seen by watching what they do.

_2_ 16. There are times when awful things happen.

3 _4_ 17. There is nothing that I must do in life.

_2_ 18. Children must eventually learn to live up to their obligations.

_3_ 19. Sometimes I just can't tolerate my poor achievement in school or at work.

3 _4_ 20. Even when I make serious or costly mistakes, or hurt others, my self-worth does not change.

_2_ 21. It would be terrible if I could not succeed at pleasing the people I love.

5 _2_ 22. I would like to do better at school (or at work) but there is no reason why I absolutely must do better.

_3_ 23. I believe that people definitely should not behave poorly in public.

_5_ 24. I just can't take a lot of pressure and stress.

25. The approval or disapproval of my friends or family does not affect my self-worth.

26. It would be unfortunate, but certainly not terrible, if someone in my family had serious medical problems.

27. I definitely have to do a good job on all things that I decide to do.

28. It's generally okay for teenagers to act differently by eating pizza for breakfast and leaving clothing and books all over the floor in their room.

29. I can't stand some of the things that have been done by my friends or members of my family.

30. A person who sins or harms others repeatedly is a "bad person."

31. It would be awful if someone I loved developed serious mental problems and had to be hospitalized.

32. I have to make absolutely sure that everything is going well in important areas of my life.

33. If it's important to me, close friends should want to do the favors that I ask of them.

34. I can easily tolerate very unpleasant situations and uncomfortable, awkward interactions with friends.

35. The way others evaluate me (friends, supervisors, teachers) is very important in determining the way I rate myself.

36. It's terrible when my friends behave poorly and inappropriately in public.

37. I clearly should not make some of the mistakes I make.

38. There is no reason why my family members must act the way I want them to.

39. It's unbearable when lots and lots of things go wrong.

___2__ 40. I often rate myself based upon my success at work or school, or upon my social achievements.

___2__ 41. It would be terrible if I totally failed in school or at work.

2 __5__ 42. There is no reason why I should be a better person than I am.

___1__ 43. There are clearly some things that other people must not do.

___2__ 44. There are some things about people at work (or in school) that I just can't stand.

___3__ 45. Serious emotional or legal problems would lower my sense of self-worth.

5 __2__ 46. Even very bad and distasteful situations like failing, or losing a lot of money or a job, are not terrible.

___2__ 47. There are some good reasons why I must not make errors at school or at work.

___3__ 48. Absolutely, my friends and family should treat me better than they sometimes do.

3 __4__ 49. I can easily accept it when my friends don't behave the way I expect them to.

___3__ 50. It is important to teach children that they can become "good boys" and "good girls" by performing well in school and earning the approval of their parents.

Reprinted with the permission of Dr. Howard Kassinove. For more information see: T. Demaria, H. Kassinove, and C. Dill (1989). "Psychometric Properties of the Survey of Rational Beliefs: A Rational-Emotive Measure of Irrational Thinking. *Journal of Personality Assessment,* 53, 329–41.

SCORING

First, you must reverse the score (1 = 6, 2 = 5, 3 = 4, 4 = 3, 5 = 2, and 6 = 1) for the following items: 1, 4, 10, 13, 17, 20, 22, 25, 26, 28, 34, 38, 42, 46, and 49. Next, you can find scores on five subscales. The names of the subscales and the items on each subscale arc as follows: Awfulizing (Aw) 1, 6, 11, 16, 21, 26, 31, 36, 41, and 46; Self-Directed Shoulds (SDS) 2, 7, 12, 17, 22, 27, 32, 37, 42, and 47; Other-Directed Shoulds (ODS) 3, 8, 13, 18, 23, 28, 33, 38, 43, and 48; Low Frustration Tolerance (LFT) 4, 9, 14, 19, 24, 29, 34, 39, 44, and 49; and Self-Worth (SW) 5, 10, 15, 20, 25, 30, 35, 40, 45, and 50. Your grand total is obtained by adding together the five subscale scores.

NORMS

Aw	SDS	ODS	LFT	SW	Total	PERCENTILE
30	31	34	35	35	165	85
28	29	32	33	33	153	70
25	26	29	30	30	140	50
22	23	26	27	27	127	30
20	21	24	25	25	115	15

(Column group heading: SCORES over Aw, SDS, ODS, LFT, SW, Total)

Handwritten annotations: "31" left of first row Aw; "32" next to SDS 31; "33" next to LFT 33; "29" next to ODS 29; "152" next to Total 153; "27" next to SW 27.

About the Survey of Personal Beliefs

The Survey of Personal Beliefs reflects an approach to psychotherapy called rational emotive therapy, developed by psychologist Albert Ellis. Ellis argued that while people tend to believe they are anxious, depressed, or otherwise unhappy because of the things that happen to them, they are really distressed by the things they say to themselves about the things that happen to them. To illustrate this distinction, suppose you go to work one morning and your boss greets you with the news that you are fired. While it may make sense to you that your bad feelings are a result of your termination and uncertain future, Ellis's response would be, "You're not depressed because you lost your job, you're depressed because of what you are saying to yourself about losing your job. You're probably telling yourself that losing your job is a tragedy, that it proves what a loser you are, and that you will never find suitable work again." Ellis would go on to tell you that it was too bad you lost your job, but it is not the end of the world. You should use the experience to learn something about yourself that will increase the odds of success on your next job. And it is doubtful that you were actually happy in a job from which you were fired, so this experience offers you the opportunity to find work that will be more satisfying. Ellis argues that to tell yourself that losing your job is a tragedy is irrational and that to feel better, you must adopt more rational, logical ways of viewing the world.

Ellis outlined numerous irrational beliefs that were especially prevalent among unhappy, distressed people, and the Survey of Personal Beliefs was developed by Howard Kassinove and Andrew Berger to reflect these common, irrational beliefs. As you can see from reading the items on this test, Ellis's list of irrational beliefs reflects a handful of common themes. One of these is that to feel worthwhile, we must be loved and approved of by virtually everyone. While most of us would agree that it is impossible for everyone to like or approve of us, many people feel genuinely devastated when they learn that a colleague or acquaintance harbors negative feelings about them. Many others will make poor decisions with the hope that it will inspire liking and approval from others. (Do the names of any politicians come to mind?) Healthy people can accept that they are disliked by others, and they are able to make the right decision even when they know it will anger some people.

A second, and in my mind an especially common irrational belief, is that all problems have good solutions. In my experience as a therapist, I have seen many clients who seek help, believing the perfect answer to their dilemma is just waiting to be found. The truth is that many problems simply do not have "good" solutions and we must settle for the least onerous alternative. The middle-aged woman married to a philanderer who is a good father and a kind companion must decide which alternative, none of which are good, works best for her. And then she must remind herself that while it is unfortunate that her husband is a womanizer, it is not the end of the world. By making the best of whatever alternative she does select, she has an excellent chance of experiencing joy and happiness again.

As you can see from the norms, we can all be a little irrational at times. While Ellis would have us believe that it is irrational to think it terrible if we failed at school or work (item 41), the average person does "Slightly Agree" with this statement. Only those people who "Totally Agree" or "Mostly Agree" are likely to end up with a score that results in their being labeled as irrational. I do like Ellis's approach to psychotherapy, but I believe there are times when he is guilty of overstating his case. I suspect the difference between people who function at a high level and others is a matter of degree. Even the best-adjusted person could be expected to feel devastated by losing a job, but they can also recover relatively quickly. They realize they have no choice but to move on and to make the best of the situation.

If you did score below the 30th percentile on this test, the odds are good that you could have a more satisfying life by modifying the things you say to yourself. The first step is to use your responses to the individual items to identify your trouble spots. Do you believe you have to be successful at everything you try in order to be worthwhile? Are you too concerned with the approval of others? Do you feel your past makes it impossible for you to find happiness? As always, the place to start is to know thine enemy.

Ellis's classic book, *A Guide to Rational Living,* is an excellent guide to help in your effort to think more rationally and logically, but the essence of this technique is to articulate these rational statements when you find you are feeling bad. So, if you feel depressed when you learn a coworker has said something nasty about you, tell yourself, "I can't please everyone. I would be a rather bland person if no one disliked me." If you feel anxious while thinking about some small problem, remind yourself that it is beyond your control and that your life is not going to be much different no matter what happens. As always, keep in mind that the key to success in making these changes is persistence and consistency.

6
How Impulsive Are You?

THE BARRATT IMPULSIVENESS SCALE

People differ in the ways they act and think in different situations. This is a test to measure some of the ways in which you act and think. Read each statement and, using the scale below, indicate how often you act and think in the way described. Do not spend too much time on any statement. Answer quickly and honestly.

4 = Almost always
3 = Often
2 = Occasionally
1 = Rarely/never

_3_ 1. I plan tasks carefully.
_2_ 2. I do things without thinking.
_2_ 3. I make up my mind quickly.
_2_ 4. I am happy-go-lucky.
_2_ 5. I don't "pay attention."
_3_ 6. I have racing thoughts.
_3_ 7. I plan trips well ahead of time.
_2_ 8. I am self-controlled.
_2_ 9. I concentrate easily.
_2_ 10. I save regularly.

_3_ 11. I squirm during plays or lectures.

_23_ 12. I am a careful thinker.

_2 3_ 13. I plan for job security.

_2_ 14. I say things without thinking.

_2 3_ 15. I like to think about complex problems.

_2_ 16. I change jobs.

_2_ 17. I act on impulse.

_2_ 18. I get easily bored when solving thought problems.

_2_ 19. I act on the spur of the moment.

3 _2_ 20. I am a steady thinker.

_2_ 21. I change where I live.

_3_ 22. I buy things on impulse.

_2_ 23. I can only think about one problem at a time.

_2_ 24. I change hobbies.

_3_ 25. I spend or charge more than I earn.

_3_ 26. I have outside thoughts when thinking.

_2_ 27. I am more interested in the present than in the future.

_3_ 28. I am restless at the theater or lectures.

2 _3_ 29. I like puzzles.

2 3 30. I am future oriented.

Reprinted with the permission of Dr. Ernest S. Barratt. For more information see: E. S. Barratt (1994). "Impulsivity: Integrating Cognitive, Behavioral, Biological, and Environmental Data." In W. B. McCown, J. L. Johnson, and M. B. Shure (Eds.): *The Impulsive Client: Theory, Research and Treatment* (pp. 39–56). Washington, D.C.: American Psychological Association.

SCORING

The scores for the following items must be reversed (4 = 1, 3 = 2, 2 = 3, and 1 = 4): 1, 7, 8, 9, 10, 12, 13, 15, 20, 29, and 30. After reversing these items, you can find your scores on three subscales as well as a total score. The first subscale is called Nonplanning and consists of items 1, 7, 8, 10, 12, 13, 14, 15, 18, 27, and 29. The second subscale is called Motor Impulsiveness and consists of items 2, 3, 4, 16, 17, 19, 21, 22, 23, 25, and 30. The third subscale is called Cognitive Impulsiveness and consists of items 5, 6, 9, 11, 20, 24, 26, and 28. Add your responses for all 30 items together for your total impulsiveness score.

NORMS

		SCORES		PERCENTILE
Nonplanning	Motor Impulsiveness	Cognitive Impulsiveness	Total	
33	25	22	75	85
30	23	20	70	70
27	21	18	65	50
24	19	16	60	30
21	17	14	55	15

About the Barratt Impulsiveness Scale

Psychologist Ernest Barratt, of the University of Texas Medical Branch, has devoted much of his career to the study of impulsiveness. Barratt became interested in this trait when he noticed that many of his clients' problems seemed to be related to their inability to resist their impulses and to plan for the future. To support his informal observations, he collected evidence that did indicate that psychiatric patients, and especially those with substance abuse problems, were likely to be impulsive people. The potential problems associated with saying "almost always" to several of the items on the test seem obvious. Clearly, someone who consistently does things without thinking, or who finds it difficult to concentrate easily, will have problems in day-to-day life. Interestingly, the relationship between some items and impulsiveness is not at all obvious. Item 4, for instance, which states, "I am happy-go-lucky," may not seem to have much to do with impulsiveness but it was included on the test because Barratt found that impulsive people were indeed more likely to endorse this item than nonimpulsive people.

One of the most important findings to emerge from Barratt's research is that impulsiveness must be considered in the context of other personality variables. To illustrate, let us consider his current area of interest, impulsive aggression. Impulsive people are not necessarily more aggressive than nonimpulsive people, but impulsive, *angry* people are likely to lash out unexpectedly. I once saw a client who fit Barratt's description like a glove. John, as I'll call him, had some problems with his impulsivity, but he was a hardworking, generally stable man. His most serious flaw was his quick temper. It was a constant struggle to keep a lid on his anger, but in most situations he was quite successful in doing so. The one important exception was any discussion with his wife in which she conveyed even the smallest hint of criticism. Whenever they would begin to talk about a problem, John would feel his anger intensifying almost immediately. He would try to remain calm, but he was like a pressure cooker with no effective release valve. Every few months he would explode; he had slapped his wife hard enough to loosen teeth, and on one occasion he pushed her down a flight of stairs, breaking her arm. John was always remorseful. He told me how much he loved his wife, how much his happiness depended on their marriage, and vowed that he would never touch her in anger again. Of course, he had made this same promise to his wife dozens of times.

By the way, nonimpulsive, angry people are fully capable of being aggressive and violent. Their acts, however, are more likely to be premeditated, and they are not especially remorseful after the episode. Impulsiveness does not cause one to be violent, but it does affect the way in which the violence is expressed.

Although Barratt was interested in the effects of being highly impulsive, I suspect that it is not necessarily desirable to have an exceptionally low score on his test either. I admit to being one of those people who is guilty of living too much in the future and not enough in the present, but some of my most valued memories are of spur-of-the-moment trips I've taken with family and friends. And think how much poorer we would be with respect to technology, literature, and art if everyone always planned for job security or never acted on impulse. I believe that my careful planning and steady thinking have generally served me well, but I sometimes wonder if these qualities have not held me back on occasion.

As the subscales on Barratt's test suggest, there are different elements to impulsiveness. We still have much to learn about the roles that Nonplanning, Motor Impulsiveness, and Cognitive Impulsiveness play in our day-to-day lives, but it seems safe to say that if you had a very high score on one or more of these dimensions, then your life would be more satisfying over the long term if you could make some adjustments. People with high scores on Nonplanning tend to live for the present with little regard for the future. It is almost impossible to have the kind of life we would like without planning how to get there. If you had a high score on this subscale, you may benefit from a more structured approach to planning your future. Write down your one-, five-, and ten-year goals. Make a list of the steps you need to take to accomplish these goals and keep records of the progress you are making.

Motor Impulsiveness seems to me to be the most problematic. High scorers are the ones who quit jobs on the spur of the moment, strike out at others when they are angry, or dig themselves a financial hole when a new credit card arrives in the mail. If you had a high score on this subscale, you must acknowledge your situation and develop effective coping strategies. Sometimes it takes only a little adjustment. I knew one college student who averaged a new job every two months. The first time her supervisor would say something that this young woman perceived as unreasonable or critical, she would walk off the job in a fit of anger. She knew she had to make a change when it became almost impossible for her to get a reference for her next job. She vowed never to walk off a job again, and only to quit after she had slept on the decision. She was able to keep her next job for eight months, and she has had a stable work history following her graduation.

John is a good example of someone with a very high score on Motor Impulsiveness. His was a very serious situation, and if you see yourself in his example, you should seek professional help immediately. (In a recent study, Barratt has found that medication may help to reduce impulsive aggression.) The consequences of such behavior are too important to ignore. John's story does not have a happy ending. Two weeks after beginning therapy, he lost his temper with his wife and pushed her against the wall. She, with the encouragement of her therapist, filed charges and moved out of the house. It was such a relief to escape John's anger that she had no interest in trying a reconciliation. If you are creating difficulties for yourself as a result of your Motor Impulsiveness, do not wait to initiate a change. Do something now.

Cognitive Impulsiveness does not seem to be a distinct category but rather something more general, and perhaps more basic. In his research, Barratt has established that certain brain patterns are associated with impulsiveness. It is too early to come to any conclusions about cause and effect, but I suspect that people who are high in cognitive impulsiveness are biologically predisposed to this pattern. If you suspect you are one of these people, perhaps the best strategy is to let your nature work to your advantage. Yes, there are some things that might be extremely difficult for you to do. You would not make a good scholar who must concentrate on dusty tomes for hours on end. But you might make a great entrepreneur who can see phenomena in a fresh light and can move quickly from task to task. You may have to guard against your tendency to act too quickly without sufficient thought, but you probably have what it takes to do things that more deliberate, cautious people (such as myself) cannot. If you recognize your limitations, you may be able to make your impulsiveness work for you rather than against you.

scale below, indicate your answer by entering it to the left of the

7

How Do You Feel about Your Body?

THE MULTIDIMENSIONAL BODY-SELF RELATIONS QUESTIONNAIRE

The following pages contain a series of statements about how people might think, feel, or behave. You are asked to indicate the extent to which each statement pertains to you personally. In order to complete the questionnaire, read each statement carefully and decide how much it pertains to you personally. Using the scale below, indicate your answer by entering it to the left of the number of the statement.

1 = Definitely disagree
2 = Mostly disagree
3 = Neither agree nor disagree
4 = Mostly agree
5 = Definitely agree

_4_ 1. Before going out in public, I always notice how I look.
_4_ 2. I am careful to buy clothes that will make me look my best.
_2_ 3. I would pass most physical-fitness tests.
_2_ 4. It is important that I have superior physical strength.
_2_ 5. My body is sexually appealing.

_1 5_ 6. I am not involved in a regular exercise program.

_2_ 7. I like my looks just the way they are.

_3_ 8. I check my appearance in a mirror whenever I can.

_4_ 9. Before going out, I usually spend a lot of time getting ready.

_2_ 10. My physical endurance is good.

_2 4_ 11. Participating in sports is unimportant to me.

2 _4_ 12. I do not actively do things to keep physically fit.

_4_ 13. Most people would consider me good-looking.

_3_ 14. It is important that I always look good.

4 _2_ 15. I use very few grooming products.

_4_ 16. I easily learn physical skills.

2 _4_ 17. Being physically fit is not a strong priority in my life.

_2_ 18. I do things to increase my physical strength.

_2_ 19. I like the way I look without my clothes.

_4_ 20. I am self-conscious if my grooming isn't right.

_2_ 21. I usually wear whatever is handy without caring how it looks.

2 _4_ 22. I do poorly in physical sports or games.

2 _4_ 23. I seldom think about my athletic skills.

_1_ 24. I work to improve my physical stamina.

_4_ 25. I like the way my clothes fit me.

4 _2_ 26. I don't care what people think about my appearance.

_4_ 27. I take special care with my hair grooming.

2 _4_ 28. I dislike my physique.

2 _4_ 29. I don't care to improve my abilities in physical activities.

_2_ 30. I try to be physically active.

2 _4_ 31. I am physically unattractive.

_3_ 32. I never think about my appearance.

_3_ 33. I am always trying to improve my physical appearance.

_3_ 34. I am very well coordinated.

_1_ 35. I play a sport regularly throughout the year.

For the following two items, place a mark by the alternative that best describes you.

_4_ 36. I think I am:

_____ 1. Very underweight

_____ 2. Somewhat underweight

_____ 3. Normal weight

_✓_ 4. Somewhat overweight

_____ 5. Very overweight

_4_ 37. From looking at me, most other people would think I am:

_____ 1. Very underweight

_____ 2. Somewhat underweight

_____ 3. Normal weight

_____ 4. Somewhat overweight

_____ 5. Very overweight

Use the scale below to indicate how satisfied you are with each of the following areas of your body:

1 = Very dissatisfied

2 = Mostly dissatisfied

3 = Neither satisfied nor dissatisfied

4 = Mostly satisfied

5 = Very satisfied

64 PERSONAL BARRIERS

___4___ 38. Face (facial features, complexion)

___3___ 39. Hair (color, thickness, texture)

___2___ 40. Lower torso (buttocks, hips, thighs, legs)

___2___ 41. Midtorso (waist, stomach)

___3___ 42. Upper torso (chest or breasts, shoulders, arms)

___2___ 43. Muscle tone

___2___ 44. Weight

___4___ 45. Height

___3___ 46. Overall appearance

Reprinted with the permission of Dr. Thomas F. Cash of Old Dominion University. For more information see: T. F. Cash (1997). *The Body Image Workbook: An 8-Step Program for Learning to Like Your Looks.* New Harbinger: Oakland, Cal. Dr. Cash has other tests related to body image available at http://www.body-images.com.

SCORING

The first step is to reverse the score (5 = 1, 4 = 2, 3 = 3, 2 = 4, and 1 = 5) for the following items: 6, 11, 12, 15, 17, 21, 22, 23, 26, 28, 29, 31, and 32. After reversing the appropriate items, you can find your score on six subscales by finding the total for the items on that scale. The subscales are: Appearance Evaluation (AE) 5, 7, 13, 19, 25, 28, and 31; Appearance Orientation (AO) 1, 2, 8, 9, 14, 15, 20, 21, 26, 27, 32, and 33; Fitness Evaluation (FE) 16, 22, and 34; Fitness Orientation (FO) 3, 4, 6, 10, 11, 12, 17, 18, 23, 24, 29, 30, and 35; Subjective Weight (SW) 36 and 37; and Body Areas Satisfaction (BAS) 38, 39, 40, 41, 42, 43, 44, 45, and 46.

NORMS

					SCORES						PERCENTILE
AE		AO		FE		FO		SW		BAS	
M	F	M	F	M	F	M	F	M	F	M	F	
30	30	51	53	14	13	55	53	8	9	45	42	85
27	27	47	51	13	12	50	48	7	8	41	38	70
24	24	43	47	11	10	44	42	6	7	37	34	50
21	21	39	43	9	8	38	36	5	6	33	30	30
18	18	35	39	8	7	33	31	4	5	29	26	15

About the Multidimensional
Body-Self Relations Questionnaire

We may pay lip service to clichés such as "you can't judge a book
by its cover," or "beauty is only skin deep," but most of us care
about how we look—more than 80 percent of us according to national surveys. These same national surveys have found that
many of us, especially women, are not very kind to ourselves
when we evaluate our appearance. About one-third of us are dissatisfied with our looks as they are, and one-half of us are dissatisfied with at least one aspect of our appearance. Psychologist
Tom Cash, who developed the test you just completed, and the
leading researcher in this area, has collected abundant evidence
showing that many people experience extreme distress about
their appearance. And this distress has far-reaching implications.
A poor body image, as researchers call these feelings, is associated with lowered satisfaction with romantic and sexual relationships and overall psychosocial adjustment. In extreme cases, a
poor body image can result in a psychological disorder called

body dysmorphic disorder. When people reach this point, they have such intense feelings of distress about their appearance that their ability to function in day-to-day life is seriously impaired. In extreme cases, people will only leave the house with most of their face covered because they are convinced they are hideously ugly.

One of Cash's most interesting findings is that for women, body image bears no relation to objective reality. It is not uncommon to find stunningly beautiful women, who earn their living as models, who feel distressed by their appearance. One such woman said, "When I look in the mirror, all I see is the flab around my thighs. I always feel surprised when I get a call to work, since I'm so sure that I'm too fat for anyone to want to photograph me again." This disconnect from objective reality also means that there are women whom others would not find especially attractive who feel good about their appearance. They do have a sense of how they rate; they would not think of applying for a job as a model. But these women can look in the mirror and feel comfortable, and even pleased, by what they see.

Men's feelings about their appearance seem to be more closely tied to objective reality. There is lots of room for exceptions, but generally if a man feels good about his appearance, others are likely to see him as attractive as well.

It comes as no surprise that women have more conflicts about their looks than men. We may not like it and even try to deny its reality, but women do tend to be judged more on their appearance than do men, especially when it comes to relationships. We may be amused but never surprised when we hear that a young, beautiful woman has married a much older Supreme Court justice, or a CEO of a major corporation. We know that men can trade their status and power for youth and beauty in a partner. On the other hand, we would be surprised if a Brad Pitt announced he was in love with a Ruth Bader Ginsberg because he found her intellect and accomplishments so impressive.

Cash found that for women, weight was the single biggest source of distress about their appearance. And society has made things especially difficult by imposing increasingly stringent standards for what an ideal body should look like. Miss America winners and *Playboy* centerfolds have both become increasingly slender over the past half century. During the 1950s, a voluptuous Marilyn Monroe–type body was considered sexy. By the 1990s, we had heroin chic. This pressure to meet such an elusive ideal takes its toll on many women. Cash found that 4 percent of women who were 20 percent below their ideal weight as determined by life insurance tables actually saw themselves as being overweight. No wonder eating disorders such as bulimia and anorexia are rampant among young women.

Our body image is something we acquire during our childhood years. I can attest to the fact that comments from family and friends during this critical period can have a lasting effect. When I was 14 years old, I had reached my full height of six foot two, but I weighed only 130 pounds. I still remember vividly one day in PE when I saw a group of girls looking my way and heard one of them say, "Look how skinny that one is." Now, nearly 30 years later, I have exceeded my ideal weight, but I still feel much more self-conscious about my skinny legs than my rounded waistline. Other people have much deeper scars. One young woman, who is quite attractive, remembers her mother's persistent advice to study hard. Since she was not as pretty as her older sister, she could not count on finding a husband to take care of her. Others were taunted by their peers for some feature such as their big ears or crooked nose, and the scars persist decades later, even though their appearance may be perfectly fine.

If there is good news about body image, it is that we seem to be kinder to ourselves as we get older. In his national survey, Cash found that people in their late adolescence and early twenties had the most negative body image, while the oldest respondents had the most positive feelings about their appearance. This shows the disconnect between our feelings and reality, since almost no one is really more attractive when they are in their sixties than their twenties. But the psychological scars do fade, and we tend to feel more comfortable about our appearance as time passes.

If your scores on the test were below the 15th percentile, especially on the Appearance Evaluation and Body Areas Satisfaction subscales, you could feel better about yourself and feel more comfortable in your romantic and sexual relationships if you developed a more positive body image. Cash has developed a self-help treatment program for this problem, to be found in his book, *The Body Image Workbook*. His approach can be called cognitive-behavioral, and it helps people to identify their distressing thoughts and teaches them to replace them with more realistic, accepting thoughts. Judy, for instance, could not stand to look at herself in the mirror when she stepped out of the shower because she was so distressed by her "fat hips and thighs"—which in reality were only slightly larger than average. She reached the point where it became increasingly difficult to perform her job as a sales representative for an office products company. She was certain that no one would listen to what she had to say because they would be repulsed by her appearance. A crucial step was for her to accept the irrationality of her conclusions. She had been successful in her job for several years, and despite her fears that others found her appearance disgusting, she continued to meet her quotas. After several sessions of therapy, she was able to look in the mirror and say more positive things to herself, including the idea that beauty is not a very good standard to use to judge oneself or others. After two months, most of her distress about making sales calls was gone. She still felt pangs of distress when she saw her image in the mirror when stepping out of the shower, but she felt confident that she could continue to make progress, as long as she persisted in her efforts to be kinder to herself. If you, like Judy, feel your life is affected by your poor body image, you can make similar changes. Remember, body image is a psychological phenomenon, and it does not necessarily reflect how others see you.

8
How Much Do You Worry?

Everybody worries from time to time. You will find below a series of statements that can apply to worrying. Please use the scale below to describe to what extent each item is characteristic of you (please write the number that describes you best in the space before each item):

5 = Entirely characteristic of me
4 = Very characteristic of me
3 = Somewhat characteristic of me
2 = A little characteristic of me
1 = Not at all characteristic of me

_1_ 1. When I worry, I feel that I am the only one to have difficulties.

_2_ 2. Worrying about less important things distracts me from more emotional subjects that I don't want to think about.

_4_ 3. If I worry, I can find a better way to be as a person.

_3_ 4. I worry because I am accustomed to worrying.

_2_ 5. I worry because I have learned to always expect the worst.

_1_ 6. I worry because if the worst happens, I would feel guilty if I hadn't worried.

_3_ 7. I worry to try to protect the world.

_4_ 8. If I worry I can find better ways to do things.

_4_ 9. I worry to try to better protect myself.

_1_ 10. If I don't worry and the worst happens, it would be my fault.

_4_ 11. I worry about the past in order to learn from my mistakes.

_2_ 12. When I worry, I think that life seems much easier for others than for me.

_4_ 13. I worry to try to have better control over my life.

_2_ 14. I worry because if the worst happens, I wouldn't be able to cope.

_4_ 15. I worry to avoid disappointment.

_4_ 16. When I worry, I tell myself that there must always be a solution to every problem.

_2_ 17. I worry about lots of little things so I won't think about more important things.

_2_ 18. By worrying, I can stop bad things from happening.

_3_ 19. Even if I know that it's not true, I feel that worrying can decrease the likelihood that the worst will happen.

_2_ 20. If I worry less, I have less chance of finding the best solution.

The following statements describe how people may react to the uncertainties of life. Please use the same five-point scale to describe to what extent each item is characteristic of you.

_3_ 21. Uncertainty stops me from having a firm opinion.

_2_ 22. Being uncertain means that a person is disorganized.

_2_ 23. Uncertainty makes life intolerable.

_4_ 24. It's not fair that there are no guarantees in life.

_2_ 25. My mind can't be relaxed if I don't know what will happen tomorrow.

_4_ 26. Uncertainty makes me uneasy, anxious, or stressed.

_3_ 27. Unforeseen events upset me greatly.

_5_ 28. It frustrates me not having all the information I need.

_4_ 29. Being uncertain allows me to foresee the consequences beforehand and to prepare for them.

_4_ 30. One should always look ahead so as to avoid surprises.

_2_ 31. A small unforeseen event can spoil everything, even with the best of planning.

_2_ 32. When it's time to act uncertainty paralyzes me.

_1_ 33. Being uncertain means that I am not first-rate.

_3_ 34. When I am uncertain, I cannot go forward.

_3_ 35. When I am uncertain, I can't function very well.

_2_ 36. Unlike me, others always seem to know where they are going with their lives.

_2_ 37. Uncertainty makes me vulnerable, unhappy, or sad.

_3_ 38. I always want to know what the future has in store for me.

_3_ 39. I hate being taken by surprise.

_2_ 40. The smallest doubt stops me from acting.

_3_ 41. I should be able to organize everything in advance.

_2_ 42. Being uncertain means that I lack confidence.

_1_ 43. I think it's unfair that other people seem sure about their future.

_2_ 44. Uncertainty stops me from sleeping well.

_2_ 45. I must get away from uncertain situations.

_2_ 46. The ambiguities in life stress me.

_4_ 47. I can't stand being undecided about my future.

Reprinted with permission of Dr. Mark H. Freeston. For more information see: M. H. Freeston, J. Rheaume, H. Letarte, M. J. Dugas, and R. LaDouceur (1994). "Why Do People Worry?" *Personality and Individual Differences,* 17, 791–802.

SCORING

You will obtain two scores for this test. By adding together your responses on the first twenty items, you will obtain your Reasons for Worrying score. By adding your responses on items 21 through 47, you will obtain your Tolerance for Uncertainty score.

NORMS

Scores		Percentile
Reasons for Worrying	*Tolerance for Uncertainty*	
90	72	
37	55	85
34	50	70
30	44	50
36	38	30
23	33	55

About the "Why Worry" Scale

One of the basic tenets of psychology is that consequences influence behavior. If we do something that makes us feel good, we are likely to do that something again in the future. And, of course, if we do something that makes us feel bad, we will try to avoid making the same mistake again. This principal, obvious as it is, does make the phenomenon of worrying difficult to understand. Worrying makes us feel bad. So how is it that some people become chronic worriers? It would seem that the unpleasant emotional consequences of worrying would be enough to motivate anyone to give it up. Psychologist Mark Freeston and his colleagues at the Université Laval in Quebec were curious about this issue, and their "Why Worry" Scale is their attempt to find some answers.

Freeston's research group based their test on the work of other theorists who have made a number of clinical observations about worriers. One such observation is that while chronic worriers are likely to agree that worrying is ultimately pointless, at some level they hold the belief that by worrying, they can reduce the likelihood of unpleasant things happening to them. As several items in the test reflect, worriers would blame themselves if something bad happened and they had not worried about it beforehand. Even though they understand the irrationality of this line of reasoning, they would feel guilty if they had been negligent in their worrying and something unfortunate occurred. Worriers may also worry to distract themselves from thinking about something even more disturbing. College students, for instance, may worry about finishing a paper on time when their real concern is whether they are bright enough to finish their degree. Worriers find it oddly comforting to fret about smaller issues because it helps them to avoid dealing with the big picture.

Worriers have also been described as hypervigilant. This means they are especially sensitive to any hint that something negative is about to happen. Fred was a chronic worrier who had no difficulty in finding things to worry about. If his boss did not say good morning with sufficient enthusiasm, it was because he was displeased with Fred's work. If Fred's fiancée did not return his phone calls within a few hours, it was because she was having second thoughts about their impending marriage. Fred, of course, made himself completely miserable by constantly looking for any sign that something bad was about to happen to him. And characteristic of worriers, Fred would interpret neutral events, such as his boss saying "good morning" in a distracted fashion, as potentially threatening.

A final clinical observation that Freeston and his colleagues used as a basis for their test is that worriers have a low tolerance for uncertainty and consequently they have difficulty in making decisions. Worriers can experience a great deal of distress over problems that do not actually exist. I know a woman who is constantly worried about the money in her retirement account. Although she has at least fifteen years until she plans to retire, she engages in endless self-debates as to whether she should shift her money from mutual funds to bonds. Her worrying is nonsensical because with her company retirement plan and her Social Security, she has more than enough money to be able to live comfortably after her retirement. Yet she allows the inherent uncertainty of the economy to cause her endless distress.

If your score was well above the 85th percentile on either subscale, you probably do experience a great deal of distress because of your worrying. So . . . what can you do about it? One line of attack lies in your score on the Reasons for Worrying subscale of the test. As Freeston and his colleagues found, if you had a high score on the Reasons for Worrying subscale, you probably had a high score on the Tolerance for Uncertainty subscale as well. Changing the way one views the world is never easy, but the odds are excellent that if you could increase your tolerance for ambiguity, you would worry less. As always, the first step is to know your enemy. Take note of how often you bemoan the uncertainty of situations. It would be a good idea to write it down, to keep a diary. Once you have a sense of the extent of the problem, you can begin to take steps to change it.

The cognitive therapy techniques that we have discussed previously can be applied to your difficulties with uncertainty. To use them, you must accept the premise that the items on the Tolerance for Uncertainty subscale represent irrational beliefs. If you cannot go this far to begin with, you must acknowledge that, at the least, they are not the best way of viewing the world.

Read the items, give yourself a lecture, and think of more productive statements that could replace the items. Rather than accepting item 23, for instance, which states that "Uncertainty makes life intolerable," try telling yourself that uncertainty makes life exciting. As a second example, replace item 33, which states that "Being uncertain means that I am not first-rate," with the more rational thought that all leaders must make decisions for which the outcome is uncertain. That's just the way life is. Again, I certainly am not suggesting that it will be easy to change the way you view life's ambiguities, but with a concerted effort you will be able to make enough of a change to make a difference in how you feel. You do not have to come to love uncertainty in order to deal with it more effectively.

A second step is to identify which of your problems are really worth worrying about. Remember, worriers often see problems when they do not exist—such as the man who worries about his job security when he receives a distracted "good morning" from his boss. Because it may be difficult for you to be objective about your worries, it would be helpful to discuss your concerns with a trusted friend. Talk about your concerns and accept your friend's guidance as to what problems are really worth worrying about.

A third step is to find more effective solutions for the problems that you do worry about. Recall the idea that worrying can serve as a substitute for even more troubling thoughts. As strange as it may sound, some worriers use their worrying as an easy way out. The student who worries about an upcoming test finds it easier to worry than to spend more time studying. The spouse who worries about being rejected may not want to make the effort to be a kinder, more loving, and more helpful partner. Yes, the problems you are worrying about may be both important and real, but the crucial issue may be finding the best solution.

It is important to keep in mind that worrying is not all bad. It can serve to motivate us to try harder, to find a better solution. So even if you scored as high as the 85th percentile, it does not necessarily mean that you have a problem. The key is to discern if you are worrying productively or needlessly. It can be difficult to draw a clear line between the adaptive and the maladaptive, but if you find yourself worrying most days, the odds are excellent that you are guilty of needless worries. The attempt to change your style is likely to be worth the effort.

SECTION II

INTERPERSONAL BARRIERS

9
How Friendly Are You?

$$\boxed{\text{THE FRIENDLINESS SCALE}}$$

The following statements are samples of how people feel about themselves and other people. There are no right or wrong answers. What is important is what you personally believe or feel is true of yourself. Read each statement carefully, then mark how much you agree or disagree with it. Indicate 4 if you agree very much. Indicate 3 if you somewhat agree. Indicate 1 if you somewhat disagree. Indicate 0 if you disagree very much.

3 ____1 1. There are many times when you don't think well of yourself.

3 ____1 2. A lot of the ideas and opinions of other people don't make much sense.

4 ____0 3. You often don't give compliments to someone who might deserve them.

1 ____3 4. You find it hard to be really yourself, even with your friends.

1 ____3 5. You are a shy person.

1 ____3 6. The ideas of your friends have little influence upon your opinions.

3 ____1 7. When your friends need advice, it is not always easy for you to give them suggestions or ideas about what to do.

1 ____3 8. You like to spend your time alone and to be by yourself.

3 ____1 9. You have many qualities that are not especially desirable.

4

____0____ 10. You don't like to be bothered by people who don't know what to do.

____4____ 11. If there is a new person around, you introduce yourself and your friends.

3

____1____ 12. The world in which we live has a lot of unfriendly people in it.

____4____ 13. You think of yourself as a person who can find something of value in any point of view.

____3____ 14. If someone comes to talk with you, you always stop whatever it is you're doing and give your attention to the person.

____0____ 15. You always lend money to people you know who ask for it.

____3____ 16. If a friend of yours moved away, you would feel sad and unhappy for quite a time.

____4____ 17. You are very pleasant and agreeable.

____4____ 18. You always listen patiently and calmly to others, even when their ideas disagree with your own.

1 ____3____ 19. Often you tell someone you're going to do something and then just forget it.

1 ____3____ 20. If you have time for fun and relaxation, you prefer to read or watch television or do something by yourself.

3 ____1____ 21. You lose your temper easily.

1 ____3____ 22. Even if you don't hear from a friend for several days and don't know why, you don't try to get in touch.

4 ____0____ 23. If you are working with people, you usually don't bother to praise them for their help.

1 ____3____ 24. Sometimes you feel all alone in the world.

1 ____3____ 25. You are not very popular.

1 ____3____ 26. When you are trying to get across your ideas, it bothers you to listen to someone who doesn't seem to know what he or she is talking about.

3 1 27. You don't go around encouraging people to get interested in hobbies, clubs, or activities.

1 3 28. People today aren't as loyal or true to one another as they used to be.

3 29. You think of yourself as a very friendly person.

3 30. It's easy for you to start a conversation with a stranger and keep it going.

3 31. When your friends are sick, you always send them a little present or give them a call.

1 32. You get invited to parties as often as you'd like.

3 33. You think of yourself as very generous.

3 34. People often come to you with their personal problems.

3 35. If you see someone needs help, you drop whatever you're doing and lend a hand.

3 36. People often take your actions and comments the wrong way.

0 4 37. You are sometimes quiet and reserved.

4 38. You make it easy for people to tell you what they think.

3 1 39. In talking with people, you mostly listen and keep your ideas and opinions to yourself.

0 4 40. Good friends are hard for you to find.

Reprinted with permission of Dr. John M. Reisman of DePaul University. For more information see: J. M. Reisman (1983). "SACRAL: Toward the Meaning and Measurement of Friendliness." *Journal of Personality Assessment, 47*, 405–13.

SCORING

The following items must be reversed (4 = 0, 3 = 1, 1 = 3, and 0 = 4): 1, 2, 3, 4, 5, 6, 7, 8, 9, 10, 12, 19, 20, 21, 22, 23, 24, 25, 26, 27, 28, 36, 37, 39, and 40. After reversing these items, change all 1s to 0. This test has four subscales: Self-Concept (S), which consists of items 1, 5, 9, 13, 17, 21, 25, 29, 33, and 37; Accessibility (AC), comprised of items 2, 6, 10, 14, 18, 22, 26, 30, 34, and 38; Rewardingness (R), comprised of items 3, 7, 11, 15, 19, 23, 27, 31, 35, and 39; and Alienation (AL), which consists of items 4, 8, 12, 16, 20, 24, 28, 32, 36, and 40. After finding your score on these four subscales, add them together for your total score.

NORMS

		SCORES			PERCENTILE
S	AC	R	AL	Total	
34	33	33	32	131	85
32	31	31	30	124	70
30	29	29	28	116	50
28	27	27	26	108	30
26	25	25	24	101	15

About the Friendliness Scale

Psychologist John Reisman was motivated to construct his test because he conceptualized friendliness slightly differently from the authors of other, similar tests. Reisman argued that existing definitions of this trait were virtually indistinguishable from other personality characteristics such as outgoingness or agreeableness. He argued that friendliness included four qualities, those represented by the subscales on his test: Self-Concept, Accessibility, Rewardingness, and Alienation. Self-Concept is important because how we view ourselves has a potent effect on our interactions with others. If we believe we have a number of undesirable qualities, or if we suspect that we do not have much to offer others, the odds are good that we will avoid interactions with them. While Reisman argues that there are exceptions, friendly people generally think of themselves as friendly people. Accessibility refers to our willingness to consider the feelings, beliefs, and opinions of others, to allow others to be a part of our lives. Rewardingness refers to our willingness to make others feel good about their interactions with us. Alienation, as the term suggests, describes people who prefer to avoid interacting with others, often because they feel these social exchanges will only make them feel worse. Reisman used these terms to form the acronym SACRAL, which is the official name he gave to his test.

Perhaps the most interesting finding of Reisman's research was that people who received low scores on his test reported having just as many friends as those who received high scores, but they were less satisfied with their friendships. And despite their having friends, they described themselves as shy and tense in social situations, and often lonely.

In an attempt to understand what distinguishes friendly from unfriendly people, Reisman asked both high and low scorers to respond to a variety of social situations. These people were asked, for example, what they would say if a friend came to them and said, "I feel like running away. What do you think I should do?" When the contents of the responses were evaluated for their appropriateness, the advice given by people who scored low on the test was judged to be as good as the advice given by high scorers. Thus, it is not the case that unfriendly people do not know what to say when interacting with others. They are as competent in this respect as friendly people. But, and this is an important *but,* Reisman found that when the style of delivery was evaluated, friendly people were judged as being significantly more positive than unfriendly people.

Reisman's research offers important hints as to the root of the problematic quality of these relationships. While Reisman showed that those with low scores do know what to say to people in different situations, their problem is instead that they do not know *how* to say the right thing.

Reisman did not speculate on how people can change this aspect of their personality, but clinicians who help clients to improve their social skills point to a number of specific changes that can be made, many of which involve nonverbal communications or body language. Perhaps the most important element is eye contact. People with low scores on the SACRAL have a poor self-concept and feel alienated from others. This keeps them from feeling confident about the worth of what they have to say, despite the fact that Reisman's research shows that their statements are likely to be as worthy as what people with high scores have to say. Their lack of confidence may cause them to avoid eye contact and to stare at the floor while they deliver their message.

There are a number of subtle, nonverbal behaviors that convey our impatience or displeasure at having to interact with another person. These cues may be difficult to specify, but they are easily recognizable. We have all met people who, even though they agree to help us, manage to physically convey their impatience or reluctance throughout the interaction. If you feel dissatisfied with your friendships, it may be that you come across this way. Along with making eye contact, make a conscious effort to communicate your interest and concern in others. Lean forward when your friends are talking to you, smile often and easily, verbalize your concern and your caring, inquire about your friend's well-being. You want everything, not just the words you use, to express your friendship.

Reisman's work offers what is, I believe, a hopeful message for those who feel dissatisfied with their friendships and their ability to be friendly. If you are one of these people, it is important to keep in mind that you have the ability to say the right thing and you have the ability to form friendships—as evidenced by Reisman's research, which shows that low scorers have just as many friends as high scorers on the SACRAL. The key to change is twofold: first, you have to change the way you view yourself, and second, you must change the expectations you have about what will happen if you extend yourself.

Reisman wrote that friendliness has its origins in early childhood. Some children attract friends easily while others, for whatever reason, are met with consistent rejection. These children later come to see themselves as not having much to offer others and as unlikable. It is not surprising that they have difficulty interacting with others in an enthusiastic way. Low scorers must work on the way they view themselves if they are to become friendlier. They have to develop confidence in their strengths, in their ability to be a good friend. If you fit in this category, you might find it useful to review the Self-Esteem chapter.

Second, you must modify your expectations of the consequences of your efforts to be friendly. You know that you can make friends, and you know the right thing to say. So as long as you express your message with the right attitude, there is no reason that others will not come to appreciate your friendship. As is always the case, as long as you make a consistent effort, you will become the sort of person who can be a valued friend.

Redo

10
How Assertive Are You?

```
┌─────────────────────────────┐
│        THE ADULT            │
│   SELF-EXPRESSION SCALE     │
└─────────────────────────────┘
```

The following inventory is designed to provide information about the way in which you express yourself. Please answer the questions by writing a number from 0 to 4 in the space to the left of each item. Your answer should indicate how you generally express yourself in a variety of situations. If a particular situation does not apply to you, answer as you think you ought to act or how you would like to act. Do not deliberate over any individual question. Your first response to the question is probably your most accurate one.

> 0 = Almost always or always
> 1 = Usually
> 2 = Sometimes
> 3 = Seldom
> 4 = Never or rarely

__3__ 1. Do you ignore it when someone pushes in front of you in line?

__2__ 2. Do you find it difficult to ask a friend to do a favor for you?

__3__ 3. If your boss or supervisor makes what you consider an unreasonable request, do you have difficultly saying no?

_3_ 4. Are you reluctant to speak to an attractive acquaintance of the opposite sex?

_4_ 5. Is it difficult for you to refuse unreasonable requests from your parents?

_3_ 6. Do you find it difficult to accept compliments from your boss or supervisor?

_3_ 7. Do you express your negative feelings to others when it is appropriate?

_3_ 8. Do you freely volunteer information or opinions in discussions with people whom you do not know well?

_2_ 9. If there was a public figure whom you greatly admired and respected at a large social gathering, would you make an effort to introduce yourself?

_4_ 10. How often do you openly express justified feelings of anger to your parents?

_4_ 11. If you have a friend of whom your parents do not approve, do you make an effort to help them get to know one another better?

_4_ 12. If you were watching a TV program in which you were very interested and a close relative was disturbing you, would you ask them to be quiet?

_3_ 13. Do you play an important part in deciding how you and your close friends spend your leisure time together?

_1_ 14. If you are angry at your spouse/boyfriend/girlfriend, is it difficult for you to tell him/her?

_3_ 15. If a friend who is supposed to pick you up for an important engagement calls fifteen minutes before he/she is supposed to be there and says that he/she cannot make it, do you express your annoyance?

_0_ 16. If in a rush you stop by a supermarket to pick up a few items, would you ask to go before someone in the checkout line?

_2_ 17. Do you find it difficult to refuse the requests of others?

_3_ 18. If your boss or supervisor expresses opinions with which you strongly disagree, do you venture to state _4_ your own point of view?

____ 19. If you have a close friend whom your spouse/boyfriend/ girlfriend dislikes and constantly criticizes, would you inform him/her that you disagree and tell him/her of your friend's assets?

_8_ 20. Do you find it difficult to ask favors of others?

_1_ 21. If food which is not to your satisfaction was served in a good restaurant, would you bring it to the waiter's attention?

_1_ 22. Do you tend to drag out your apologies?

_1_ 23. When necessary, do you find it difficult to ask favors of your parents?

_3_ 24. Do you insist that others do their fair share of the work?

_0_ 25. Do you have difficulty saying no to salesmen?

_0_ 26. Are you reluctant to speak up in a discussion with a small group of friends?

_3_ 27. Do you express anger or annoyance to your boss or supervisor when it is justified?

_3_ 28. Do you compliment and praise others?

_2_ 29. Do you have difficulty asking a close friend to do an important favor, even though it will cause him/her some inconvenience?

_0_ 30. If a close relative makes what you consider to be an unreasonable request, do you have difficulty saying no?

____ 31. If your boss or supervisor makes a statement that you consider untrue, do you question it aloud?

____ 32. If you find yourself becoming fond of a friend, do you have difficulty expressing these feelings to that person?

_____33. Do you have difficulty exchanging a purchase with which you are dissatisfied?

_____34. If someone in authority interrupts you in the middle of an important conversation, do you request that the person wait until you have finished?

_____35. If a person of the opposite sex whom you have been wanting to meet directs attention to you at a party, do you take the initiative in beginning the conversation?

_____36. Do you hesitate to express resentment to a friend who has unjustifiably criticized you?

_____37. If your parents wanted you to come home for a weekend visit and you had made important plans, would you change your plans?

_____38. Are you reluctant to speak up in a discussion or debate?

_____39. If a friend who has borrowed $5.00 from you seems to have forgotten about it, is it difficult for you to remind this person?

_____40. If your boss or supervisor teases you to the point that it is no longer fun, do you have difficulty expressing your displeasure?

_____41. If your spouse/boyfriend/girlfriend is blatantly unfair, do you find it difficult to say something about it to him/her?

_____42. If a clerk in a store waits on someone who has come in after you when you are in a rush, do you call his attention to the matter?

_____43. If you lived in an apartment and the landlord failed to make certain repairs after it had been brought to his attention, would you insist on it?

_____44. Do you find it difficult to ask your boss or supervisor to let you off early?

_____45. Do you have difficulty verbally expressing love and affection to your spouse/boyfriend/girlfriend?

_____ 46. Do you readily express your opinions to others?

_____ 47. If a friend makes what you consider to be an unreasonable request, are you able to refuse?

Reprinted with the permission of Dr. John P. Galassi. For more information see:
M. L. Gay, J. G. Hollandsworth, and J. P. Galassi (1975). "An Assertiveness Inventory for Adults." *Journal of Counseling Psychology,* 22, 340–44.

SCORING

The first step in scoring is to reverse score (4 = 0, 3 = 1, 2 = 2, 1 =
3, and 0 = 4) the following items: 7, 8, 9, 10, 11, 12, 13, 15, 16, 18,
19, 21, 24, 27, 28, 31, 34, 35, 42, 43, 44, 46, and 47. Then simply
add together your responses to all of the items. Higher scores
indicate higher levels of assertiveness.

NORMS

SCORE		PERCENTILE
Men	*Women*	
138	137	85
129	126	70
119	115	50
109	104	30
100	93	15

About the Adult Self-Expression Scale

Assertiveness, defined as the socially appropriate expression of feelings, is extremely important to having effective interpersonal interactions. This very important quality has interested behavioral psychologists for decades, and they have developed a variety of tests to measure it. One of the best of these is the Adult Self-Expression Scale created by psychologists Melvin Gay, James Hollandsworth, and John Galassi.

People who are low in assertiveness are likely to have at least two problem areas. First, they cut themselves off from others. They have difficulty approaching others to make that crucial first contact. When they are approached, they may feel at a loss for words and fail to convey their interest in the person. When they do manage to make contact with another person, they may be reluctant to express their true feelings, even when their feelings are extremely positive. Their lack of assertiveness often results in their feeling lonely and isolated.

The second problem nonassertive people have is that they allow others to take advantage of them. As several of the items on the test suggest, these people are reluctant to object when a friend makes an unreasonable request, they accept criticism and hurtful remarks without objection, they allow others to infringe on their plans. Often these nonassertive people will rationalize their failure to object to the selfishness of others by saying to themselves that it's not worth the risk of creating ill will. What they do not understand, however, is that their failure to assert themselves is indeed creating ill will—in themselves. The person who justifies his failure to refuse a friend's unreasonable requests by saying, "It's a small thing, I don't want to make anyone mad," will end up being the one who is mad. It is possible to overlook one, two, maybe even a half-dozen unreasonable requests, but sooner or later they will take their toll. The nonassertive person will begin to resent these demanding friends, and because this person finds it impossible to say what is on his or her mind, he or she will gradually withdraw from them, since it is the only available strategy for dealing with the smoldering resentment and hostility. If your score was below the 30th percentile, you would probably feel much better about your relationships with other people if you became a more assertive person.

The first step to becoming more assertive is to discard your rationalizations that are holding you back. Most nonassertive people confuse assertiveness with aggressiveness. By definition, assertiveness is socially appropriate, whereas aggressiveness can be offensive and even cruel. Aggressive people may use their personality to intimidate others, or exert an unfair influence. Assertive people say what is on their mind in a socially appropriate way and refuse to allow others to take advantage of them. To tell a friend that you do not like it when he or she is a half hour late is not being aggressive, it is being assertive. To tell a friend no when he or she asks to borrow your car for the weekend even though it means you will be housebound is not petty mean-spiritedness, but a perfectly appropriate refusal of an inappropriate request. Remember, being assertive does not necessarily mean raising your voice or saying cruel things, it merely means being clear about what you are thinking and feeling.

To illustrate how one can learn to be assertive, let me describe a former client whom I'll call Sam. Sam was a junior in college, and even though he was a good-looking, bright kid, he had never had a date. He was desperately lonely, but he was terrified by the prospect of even talking to a girl. My first assignment for Sam was simply to make eye contact with girls and smile as he walked around campus. Sam was so low in assertiveness that it took him a full week before he could do it and another week before he could feel comfortable while doing it. When he arrived for the following session, he was genuinely surprised by the reaction he got. "Most of the girls I smiled at actually smiled back," he reported.

The next assignment was to add a friendly "hi" to his smile. This came easier for him, and this simple, basic human contact was enough to significantly reduce his feelings of loneliness.

In the following sessions we began to role-play what he might say when asking a girl for a date, but we never had a chance to test my suggestions. While waiting for the elevator one day, a girl that he had said hello to several times initiated a conversation with him. They got on the elevator together, and before they reached the ground floor, she invited him to have a cup of coffee! Yes, Sam's situation was somewhat unusual in that it changed so quickly, but it is not unusual in the end results. Once people begin to make small increases in their assertiveness, they feel so gratified by the results that it becomes easier to make subsequent changes.

Sam's situation was such that it was easy for him to practice making small changes before moving on to more substantial changes. There are times, however, when you must give all or nothing. Let me tell you about Judy, another former client. She was having problems with her roommate, who borrowed money frequently but never remembered to pay it back. Judy felt she would be petty to say no since the "loans" were always small. It took some time to convince her that her roommate was the one guilty of pettiness and that Judy's annoyance was to be expected. We talked about various ways Judy could express her feelings and then role-played her answer for the next time her roommate asked for a loan. Judy did tell her roommate that she would not lend her any money because the roommate never paid it back, and as Judy expected, her roommate was miffed. But Judy came to see how ludicrous the situation was—that she was feeling bad when in fact it was her roommate who should feel embarrassed.

In my experience, increasing one's assertiveness is one change that, relatively speaking, is easy to make. The rewards for making small changes are so immediate and so obvious that people are eager to move to the next step. Good luck with your first step.

11

How Capable Are You of Intimacy?

THE FEAR OF
INTIMACY SCALE

PART A INSTRUCTIONS: Imagine you are in a close, dating relationship. Respond to the following statements as you would if you were in that close relationship. Rate how characteristic each statement is of you on a scale of 1 to 5 as described below. Note that in each statement "X" refers to the person who would be in the close relationship with you.

> 1 = Not at all characteristic of me
> 2 = Slightly characteristic of me
> 3 = Moderately characteristic of me
> 4 = Very characteristic of me
> 5 = Extremely characteristic of me

_____ 1. I would feel uncomfortable telling X about things in the past that I have felt ashamed of.

_____ 2. I would feel uneasy talking with X about something that has hurt me deeply.

_____ 3. I would feel comfortable expressing my true feelings to X.

_____ 4. If X were upset I would sometimes be afraid of showing that I care.

_____ 5. I might be afraid to confide my innermost feelings to X.

_____ 6. I would feel at ease telling X that I care about him/her.

_____ 7. I would have a feeling of complete togetherness with X.

_____ 8. I would be comfortable discussing significant problems with X.

_____ 9. A part of me would be afraid to make a long-term commitment to X.

_____ 10. I would feel comfortable telling X my experiences, even sad ones.

_____ 11. I would probably feel nervous showing X strong feelings of affection.

_____ 12. I would find it difficult being open with X about my personal thoughts.

_____ 13. I would feel nervous showing X strong feelings of affection.

_____ 14. I would not be afraid to share with X what I dislike about myself.

_____ 15. I would be afraid to take the risk of being hurt in order to establish a closer relationship with X.

_____ 16. I would feel comfortable keeping very personal information to myself.

_____ 17. I would not be nervous about being spontaneous with X.

_____ 18. I would feel comfortable telling X things that I do not tell other people.

_____ 19. I would feel comfortable trusting X with my deepest thoughts and feelings.

_____ 20. I would sometimes feel uneasy if X told me about very personal matters.

_____ 21. I would be comfortable revealing to X what I feel are my shortcomings and handicaps.

_____ 22. I would be comfortable with having a close emotional tie between us.

_____23. I would be afraid of sharing my private thoughts with X.

_____24. I would be afraid that I might not always feel close to X.

_____25. I would be comfortable telling X what my needs are.

_____26. I would be afraid that X would be more invested in the relationship than I would be.

_____27. I would feel comfortable about having open and honest communication with X.

_____28. I would sometimes feel uncomfortable listening to X's personal problems.

_____29. I would feel at ease to completely be myself around X.

_____30. I would feel relaxed being together and talking about our personal goals.

PART B INSTRUCTIONS: Respond to the following statements as they apply to your past relationships. Rate how characteristic each statement is of you on a scale of 1 to 5 as described in the instructions for Part A.

_____31. I have shied away from opportunities to be close to someone.

_____32. I have held my feelings back in previous relationships.

_____33. There are people who think that I am afraid to get close to them.

_____34. There are people who think that I am not an easy person to get to know.

_____35. I have done things in previous relationships to keep me from developing closeness.

Reprinted with permission of Dr. Carol J. Descutner. For more information see: C. J. Descutner and M. H. Thelen (1991). "Development and Validation of a Fear-of-Intimacy Scale." *Psychological Assessment,* 3, 218–25.

SCORING

The first step is to reverse your score (5 = 1, 4 = 2, 3 = 3, 2 = 4, and 1 = 5) for the following items: 3, 6, 7, 8, 10, 14, 17, 18, 19, 21, 22, 25, 27, 29, and 30. Then simply add your responses for the 35 items.

NORMS

SCORE		PERCENTILE
Men	Women	
103	99	85
93	88	70
82	76	50
71	64	30
61	53	15

About the Fear of Intimacy Scale

The ability to connect with others has its own, obvious satisfactions, but it also serves to promote mental health. Research psychologists have established that people who have the capacity to be intimate with others have more satisfying relationships with friends, family, and colleagues, and fewer emotional difficulties than those who do not have this ability. University of Missouri psychologists Carol Descutner and Mark Thelen constructed the Fear of Intimacy Scale with the hope that it would be useful to both clinicians and researchers to identify those people whose anxieties about being intimate with others may interfere with their ability to form satisfying relationships and their mental well-being.

Descutner and Thelen gathered evidence that demonstrates that people with high scores on their scale do have a number of intimacy problems. Compared to low scorers, they acknowledge that others find it difficult to get to know them, they have had fewer relationships lasting more than a couple of months, they are less satisfied with the quality of their dating relationships, they feel uncomfortable at the prospect of getting close to others, and they do not expect to feel satisfied once they enter a long-term relationship or marriage. Given these problems, it is not surprising that people with a fear of intimacy are significantly lonelier than their counterparts.

I was surprised, but pleased, by the findings that men and women scored similarly on their test. There is an abundance of research evidence suggesting that men are less likely than women to reveal their innermost feelings. Indeed, Ronald Levant, a Harvard Medical School professor, has coined the term "normative male alexithymia" (sounds serious, doesn't it), an inability to put feelings into words, to reflect his belief that this is a pervasive problem for men. And a number of mental health professionals have made men's purported problems with intimacy a cottage industry. It is not difficult to conclude that the mental health profession views men as, to use a politically correct term, intimacy impaired.

I was pleased by the finding that men and women have similar scores on the Fear of Intimacy Scale because it is consistent with the way I think about this issue. I do believe that men are less likely to talk about their innermost feelings than are women, but I do not believe this represents a fear of intimacy. It may instead reflect a lack of interest, or it may reflect a preference for alternative ways of dealing with bad feelings. Richard and Janet, a couple I saw in therapy, had many discussions along these lines. "Richard won't talk to me or share his feelings with me," Janet would complain. Richard, on the other hand, had a very different perspective. "I don't understand how she could think that. When I have a bad day at work, I tell her what happened. When we have a problem with one of our kids, I tell her how sad, angry, whatever, I feel about it. She wants to talk about these things for hours and hours, and I can't stand doing that."

As everyone who has seen a "Men Are from Mars . . ." info-mercial knows, women do seem to gain comfort from discussing their feelings in detail. When Janet had a problem at work, she found it comforting to share all the details with her husband. When Richard had a similar problem, he found it comforting to give a bare-bones sketch of the situation to Janet, but then he wanted to move on and talk about something more pleasant. Talking about his problem in detail was too much like reliving it for Richard. Men do tend to be more solution-focused than women, and Richard had learned (the info-mercials were enough for him) that Janet did not appreciate his suggestions when she discussed her problems at work, she simply wanted to talk. Janet had to learn that Richard's reluctance to discuss his feelings in greater detail did not represent his unwillingness to share his life with her, but was a different way of dealing with conflict—not necessarily a better way or an inferior way, simply a different way. The point is that women should not be too quick to assume that men have a fear of intimacy.

If you did receive a high score on this test, it probably is the case that you could improve your relationships and your overall satisfaction with life by working on your communication skills. Psychologist Spencer Rathus has made a number of recommen-dations for those who wish to increase their ability to be emo-tionally intimate. A first step is to "talk about talking" — to share with your partner how difficult it is to talk about certain issues. You might even ask your partner for help in discussing issues that are difficult for you to bring up. You might say, "There is some-thing I would like to talk to you about, but I'm not sure how to get started. Can you help me?"

Rathus points out that listening can be as important to inti-macy as talking and has made several suggestions for improving these skills. He recommends that people be "active listeners," that they maintain an appropriate level of eye contact while their partner is talking, that they express their understanding through body language and facial gestures, and that they ask for clarification and elaboration when appropriate.

While such techniques can be quite useful, I suspect that most people who have difficulty achieving intimacy know what to say, but they are afraid to say it. There is a real risk that, should we bare our soul, it could come back to haunt us. Most of us have had at least one experience of telling a close friend a deep, dark secret only to learn later that it was no longer such a secret, that our friend had betrayed us. While those with a fear of intimacy may vow never to make that mistake again, a better strategy, and one that comes naturally to most people, is to build intimacy gradually, to learn from experience if you can trust this other person.

Sharing one's innermost feelings can also be scary because it makes one vulnerable. *Seinfeld,* a show that captured so many relationship issues so well, devoted one show to George's dilemma as to whether he should tell the woman he was dating that he loved her. He expressed his concerns to Jerry when he said, "But if she doesn't say 'I love you' back, I'm left hanging out there." George's worst fears came true, but true to life, he survived. Yes, he felt humiliated, and yes, he did not know how he could continue to see the woman when she made it clear she did not feel the same about him, but he survived. As time goes on and we gain more experience, these minor humiliations do seem very minor indeed. It is far more likely for people to regret passing up an opportunity for intimacy than to dwell on any embarrassment they may have felt similar to George's.

12
Are You a Controlling Person?

THE WAY OF
LIFE SCALE

The following questionnaire should be filled out according to how you feel at the present. Respond with a "True" or a "False" depending on which choice *most accurately* describes you.

_____ 1. I am easily awakened by noise.

_____ 2. When it's time to make a major decision like purchasing a house or a car, I usually make that decision.

_____ 3. When it's time to make a major decision about moving, I usually make that decision.

_____ 4. My daily life is full of things that are interesting.

_____ 5. I enjoy detective or mystery stories.

_____ 6. I work under a great deal of tension.

_____ 7. When it's time to discipline the children, I make that decision.

_____ 8. No one seems to understand me.

_____ 9. When it's time to decide about social events with friends or family, I usually make that decision.

_____10. I like to be bossy.

_____11. At times I feel like swearing.

_____12. I like to get in the last word.

_____13. I find it hard to keep my mind on a task.

_____14. At times I feel like smashing things.

_____15. I like to know the details about other people's phone conversations.

_____16. I do not always tell the truth.

_____17. I like to have rules and structure for handling most or all situations.

_____18. I like to monitor other people to make sure things are going the way they should be.

_____19. I like to make sure everything goes according to plan.

_____20. I am a good mixer.

_____21. I like to lead conversations or group discussions.

_____22. I am liked by most people.

_____23. I get angry sometimes.

_____24. I may be inclined to interrupt people if they are not responding in the way they should be.

_____25. I think most people would lie to get ahead.

_____26. I am lacking in self-confidence.

_____27. I am an important person.

_____28. I have a tendency to manipulate, maneuver, or control other people.

_____29. I am a good leader but not particularly a good follower.

_____30. I like to give directions about driving or other activities.

_____31. I am happy most of the time.

_____32. I am a person who, if I am going out for an evening, likes to decide where to eat, what movie to attend, etc.

_____33. My hardest battles are with myself.

_____34. I seem to be about as capable and smart as most others around me.

_____35. I tend to overstructure spontaneous time such as vacation, etc. and turn them into controlled events.

_____36. I feel useless at times.

_____37. I have ideas about controlling other things with the children and other people such as how much food they should have on their plate, etc.

_____38. I am seen by relatives as being a dominant member of our extended family.

_____39. I am the one who usually decides which television channel to watch.

_____40. I am the one who usually controls the thermostat in the house.

_____41. Criticism or scolding hurts me terribly.

_____42. I would rather win than lose in a game.

_____43. I do not tire quickly.

Reprinted with permission of Dr. Logan Wright of the University of Oklahoma. For more information see: L. Wright, K. von Bussmann, A. Freidman, M. Khoury, and F. Owens (1990). "Exaggerated Social Control and Its Relationship to the Type A Behavior Pattern." *Journal of Research in Personality,* 24, 258–69.

SCORING

The Way of Life Scale uses a technique that, while common in test construction, is one we have not seen in the other tests in this book—it uses a number of "distractor items" to disguise the purpose of the test. So, while 43 items appear on the scale, only 21 of the items are actually relevant to the purpose of the test. To find your score, count the number of "True" responses to items 2, 3, 7, 9, 10, 12, 15, 17, 18, 19, 21, 24, 28, 29, 30, 32, 35, 37, 38, 39, and 40.

NORMS

Score	Percentile
15	85
13	70
11	50
9	30
7	15

About the Way of Life Scale

University of Oklahoma psychologist Logan Wright and his colleagues constructed the Way of Life Scale to learn more about the Type A personality—a term that has made its way from the research laboratory to popular jargon in a remarkably short time. Type A personalities are described as ambitious, impatient, hard-driving, time-pressured, and hostile people. This personality type burst into the public consciousness some thirty years ago when researchers discovered that such people were prone to coronary heart disease.

Wright and his colleagues noted that while a variety of elements come together to form the Type A personality, not all of these qualities are bad, or "toxic," to use their term. In fact, people with Type A personalities tend to be more successful in their academic and vocational careers than their Type B counterparts. Furthermore, Type As are quicker to recognize hopeless, no-win situations than are Type Bs. There are some good things about being a Type A, but it can be difficult for these people to retain the good while ridding themselves of the toxic components.

Over the past few years, a number of researchers have collected impressive evidence that anger and hostility are the components of the Type A personality that are especially troublesome (see chapter 13). Wright and his colleagues wondered if an exaggerated need for social control, also referred to as "nonmutuality," might also be one of the toxic elements. To learn if this might be true, they developed the test you just completed, the Way of Life Scale. As you could tell from the scoring system, only 21 of the items are used to derive the score. The remaining 22 items are "distractor" items to make the nature of the test less obvious to those taking it. This is sometimes done because if people know what a test is intended to measure, they may respond in such a way so as to produce a desirable score.

Wright did find that there was a relationship between scores on his Way of Life Scale and Type A personality in a group of patients recovering from coronary heart disease. As he pointed out, additional research is needed before we can conclude cause and effect, but it seems likely that this exaggerated need for social control or nonmutuality is one of the toxic components of the Type A personality.

I was fascinated by this test because one of the most common complaints I hear in therapy from both men and women about their spouses is that they are too "controlling." While this is another psychological term that is widely used by laypeople, Wright's test represents one of very few attempts to measure this quality—one that can be highly toxic to relationships. People with high scores on this test are indeed likely to have resentful partners. Not only do they want to make the big decisions, such as where to live or how to discipline the children, but they also assume control over the trivial—what movie to see, what to have for dinner, where to set the thermostat. When working on a task, controlling people are reluctant to defer to their partner, even when it is clear their partner has superior ability. No wonder these people are so hard to live with.

If you had a high score on this test, the odds are good that your partner feels resentful about your need to always have things go your way. And unless you can change your ways, your relationship is in for some difficult times. Although we have much to learn about this personality trait, your relationships with friends and colleagues are probably hurt by your need to control them as well. High scorers' pervasive need to be "in control" makes them insensitive to the needs, feelings, and opinions of others. High scorers are even unwilling to share the conversational ball; they need to control that as well. It is often difficult for controlling people to see their situation clearly, but they give up the opportunity for warm, caring relationships by demanding to always be in charge.

If you score highly on this test, it will not be easy for you to change your ways. Even those who have experienced coronary heart disease find it difficult to tone down their personalities, even though they know it may mean the difference between life and death. I believe the first step is to attempt to fully understand how your need to be in control is affecting your relationships with others. Talk openly with your partner and your friends. Invite them to share with you their feelings about your behavior. Expect them to be reluctant about being candid: your anger is intimidating. Understand that their criticisms will elicit an intense urge on your part to justify your actions. Be calm and patient, and listen to all they have to say.

Once you are ready to make some changes, begin with the small stuff. Ask a child to build a tower of blocks or put together a model without interfering. Yes, you could probably improve on the child's effort, but remember, that is not the point. Ask your partner to pick a restaurant and movie for the evening and go along with the plans cheerfully. Do not offer your thoughts about the bad review you read, for instance; simply give up control for a single evening.

Recognize that there may be some situations in which it will be almost impossible for you to give up control. In other words, do not pretend that you and your partner are going to plant a garden together if you find it intolerable not to do it your way. If you must, plant your own garden and allow your partner to plant his or her own.

It will be difficult to change and it will take an enormous amount of self-discipline, but the rewards are great. Not only will you increase your odds of living a long, healthy life, but you also will discover the richness of human relationships when they are based on mutuality and respect. Don't give up.

13
Are You an Angry Person?

THE MULTIDIMENSIONAL ANGER INVENTORY

Everybody gets angry from time to time. A number of statements that people have used to describe the times they get angry are included below. Use the guidelines below to indicate how well each of the following statements describes you. Please answer every item.

5 = Completely true
4 = Mostly true
3 = Partly false/partly true
2 = Mostly false
1 = Completely false

_____ 1. I tend to get angry more frequently than most people.

_____ 2. Other people seem to get angrier than I do in similar circumstances.

_____ 3. I harbor grudges that I don't tell anyone about.

_____ 4. I try to get even when I'm angry with someone.

_____ 5. I am secretly quite critical of others.

_____ 6. It is easy to make me angry.

_____ 7. When I am angry with someone, I let that person know.

_____ 8. I have met many people who are supposed to be experts who are no better than I.

_____ 9. Something makes me angry almost every day.

_____ 10. I often feel angrier than I think I should.

_____ 11. I feel guilty about expressing my anger.

_____ 12. When I am angry with someone, I take it out on whoever is around.

_____ 13. Some of my friends have habits that annoy and bother me very much.

_____ 14. I am surprised at how often I feel angry.

_____ 15. Once I let people know I'm angry, I can put it out of my mind.

_____ 16. People talk about me behind my back.

_____ 17. At times, I feel angry for no specific reason.

_____ 18. I can make myself angry about something in the past just by thinking about it.

_____ 19. Even after I have expressed my anger, I have trouble forgetting about it.

_____ 20. When I hide my anger from others, I think about it for a long time.

_____ 21. People can bother me just by being around.

_____ 22. When I get angry, I stay angry for hours.

_____ 23. When I hide my anger from others, I forget about it pretty quickly.

_____ 24. I try to talk over problems with people without letting them know I'm angry.

_____ 25. When I get angry, I calm down faster than most people.

_____ 26. I get so angry, I feel like I might lose control.

_____ 27. If I let people see the way I feel, I'd be considered a hard person to get along with.

_____ 28. I am on my guard with people who are friendlier than I expected.

____29. It's difficult for me to let people know I'm angry.

____30. I get angry when:

    ____ a. Someone lets me down.

    ____ b. People are unfair.

    ____ c. Something blocks my plans.

    ____ d. I am delayed.

    ____ e. Someone embarrasses me.

    ____ f. I have to take orders from someone less capable than I.

    ____ g. I have to work with incompetent people.

    ____ h. I do something stupid.

    ____ i. I am not given credit for something I have done.

Reprinted with permission of Dr. Judith M. Siegel. For more information see: J. M. Siegel (1986). "The Multidimensional Anger Inventory." *Journal of Personality and Social Psychology,* 51, 191–200.

SCORING

The first step in scoring is to reverse (5 = 1, 4 = 2, 3 = 3, 2 = 4, and 1 = 5) the following items: 2, 23, and 25. Next, you can find your score on five subscales. Please note that some items appear on more than one subscale. The first is Anger Arousal and consists of items 1, 2, 5, 6, 9, 10, 14, 17, 18, 21, 22, 25, and 26. The second dimension is Range of Anger-Eliciting Situations and includes items 30a, 30b, 30c, 30d, 30e, 30f, 30g, 30h, and 30i. The third dimension is Hostile Outlook and consists of items 8, 13, 17, 18, 21, 22, 28, 30a, 30b, 30f, 30g, and 30i. The fourth dimension is Anger-Out and consists of items 7, 23, 24, and 29. And the fifth dimension is Anger-In and consists of items 3, 4, 11, 19, 20, and 27.

NORMS

SCORES						PERCENTILE
AA	RAS	HO	AO	AI	Total	
47	33	44	14	22	160	85
42	29	39	13	20	142	70
36	25	34	11	17	123	50
30	21	29	9	14	104	30
25	17	24	8	12	86	15

About the Multidimensional Anger Inventory

As is the case with all sciences, psychology has been guilty of its share of mistakes. One interesting example of this concerns the emotion of anger. For many years, the common wisdom was that people should express their anger, that it was unhealthy to suppress it. Freud, one of the first proponents of this view, argued that depression is anger turned inward, so clearly, it would be better to express one's anger outward to avoid the negative consequences of repressing it. This belief was strengthened in the 1950s when psychoanalyst Franz Alexander wrote that pent-up anger would intensify, resulting in a chronic emotional state that caused hypertension. Alexander's theory received some support in the 1960s when a group of researchers brought people into the laboratory and deliberately made them angry, which caused their blood pressure to increase. Half of these research participants were subsequently allowed to retaliate against the person who made them angry, and for these people, there was a decrease in their blood pressure. So, it seemed clear: expressing anger could lower one's blood pressure and possibly preclude the risk of coronary heart disease.

Now, nearly 40 years later, researchers have a very different view of anger, and it appears as if there is very little that is good about it. As is always the case, the situation is extremely complex and the interplay of a number of variables must be considered, but it does appear that anger poses serious health and social risks. Perhaps the most dramatic illustration of the health risks was presented by a group of researchers from the University of North Carolina who gave a group of medical students a test measuring their hostility. Twenty-five years later, physicians who had been high in hostility as students were significantly more likely not only to have suffered coronary disease but also to have died!

The social risks of anger have been well publicized over the past several years. Who has not heard of ugly and tragic incidents stemming from road rage? Both spouse and child abuse are almost always preceded by the perpetrator experiencing anger. Over the past half century, we psychologists have gone from teaching people how to express their anger to leading anger management seminars. Anger is something that is best controlled.

UCLA psychologist Judith Siegel developed the Multidimensional Anger Inventory to reflect the complexity of the emotion of anger. After reviewing the scientific literature dealing with the relationship between anger and coronary heart disease, she noted that there are a number of dimensions associated with this dangerous emotion. As the scales on her test suggest, some people may become angry often, but a relatively narrow range of situations elicit their anger. Other people may have a generally hostile outlook on the world, even though they may not experience a great deal of emotional intensity when they feel angry. Siegel's goal was to develop a test that would help researchers better understand exactly what components of anger contribute to coronary heart disease.

While we still have much to learn about the precise nature of anger, it is clear that if you received high scores on this test then you would benefit from modifying your anger level. It is never easy to change lifelong patterns, but the evidence is clear that anger management programs work. It is true that some of us are predisposed by our biological makeup to respond more strongly than others, but the experience of anger is strongly influenced by learning. If we observed our parents becoming angry frequently, we learned that anger is an expected reaction in such situations. And remember, patterns that are learned can be unlearned.

Perhaps the most important step in modifying your anger is to recognize that it is under your control. Too many angry people blame the target of their emotions. The abusive husband blames his wife for provoking him. The woman who experiences road rage blames stupid and incompetent drivers. If you want to change, you have to accept responsibility for your reactions. You cannot blame others for the emotions you experience. You are in charge, and it is up to you to do something about your anger.

One important step in modifying your anger is to learn a more appropriate, healthier response to situations that make you angry. Most anger management programs use relaxation training to help people with this step. A good source of additional information about the benefits of relaxation and detailed instructions to help you learn this response is Harvard psychiatrist Herbert Benson's book, *The Relaxation Response.* Even if you do not spend the time to thoroughly master these techniques, you can accomplish a great deal with very simple breathing exercises. Suppose you are stuck in traffic and know you will be late to an important meeting. Rather than feel angry at all the "idiots" who are making life difficult for you, simply lean back in your seat, take several slow, deep breaths, and repeat the word *relax* to yourself. This will not work miracles the first time you try it, but if you consistently practice relaxing in situations that typically make you angry, you will be surprised by the change in yourself over a few weeks' time.

Along with learning to relax, you must change your thoughts. I do not have much of a problem with anger but there is one situation that I have had to make a conscious effort to work on— the express line in the grocery store. I would find myself becoming increasingly angry when the people in front of me did not do everything they could to make the line move quickly. Especially infuriating was the person who would wait until the checker announced the total before digging through her purse to find her pocketbook. Then, this especially annoying person would dig through her change pocket to preserve as many of her precious dollar bills as possible (see, I'm getting worked up just writing about it). I decided I had to change when I realized I would still be angry by the time I got home from the store. So I would take the deep breaths and then tell myself that at most, it was adding a minute to my delay and that the woman was not intentionally doing this to make my life miserable. And rather than stare at her in a futile attempt to speed her up, I would amuse myself by reading the headlines of the tabloid newspapers that are always adjacent to the checkout line.

It has been several years since I vowed to work on this, and there are still times when I am in a hurry and I have to remind myself to practice what I preach. It is almost impossible to completely change our reactions, but it is also true that I almost never walk out of the store feeling angry at the people who were ahead of me in line. With persistence, you too can overcome most anything.

14
How Trusting Are You?

THE SPECIFIC INTERPERSONAL
TRUST SCALE

The following statements concern opinions and feelings that you may hold toward another person. With respect to another specific person in whom you have a great deal of trust (designated as X), indicate the extent to which you agree or disagree with each statement by writing in the number that best expresses your opinion or feeling according to the key below. Note that there are separate versions of the test for men and women.

1 = Very strongly disagree
2 = Disagree
3 = Moderately disagree
4 = Slightly disagree
5 = Neither agree nor disagree
6 = Slightly agree
7 = Moderately agree
8 = Agree
9 = Strongly agree

ITEMS FOR MEN

_____ 1. If X gave me a compliment I would question if X really meant what was said.

_____ 2. If we decided to meet somewhere for lunch, I would be certain X would be there.

_____ 3. I would go hiking with X in unfamiliar territory if X assured me that he/she knew the area.

_____ 4. I wouldn't want to buy a piece of furniture from X because I wouldn't believe his/her estimate of its worth.

_____ 5. I would expect X to play fair.

_____ 6. I could rely on X to mail an important letter for me if I couldn't get to the post office.

_____ 7. I would be able to confide in X and know that he/she would want to listen.

_____ 8. I could expect X to tell the truth.

_____ 9. If I had to catch an airplane, I could not be sure X would get me to the airport in time.

_____ 10. If X unexpectedly laughed at something I did or said, I would wonder if he/she was being critical and unkind.

_____ 11. I could talk freely to X and know that X would want to listen.

_____ 12. X would never intentionally misrepresent my point of view to others.

_____ 13. If X knew what kinds of things hurt my feelings, I would never worry that he/she would use them against me.

_____ 14. I would be able to confide in X and know that he/she would want to listen.

_____ 15. If X didn't think I had handled a certain situation very well, he/she would not criticize me in front of other people.

_____ 16. If I told X what things I worry about, he/she would not think my concerns were silly.

_____ 17. If my alarm clock was broken and I asked X to call me at a certain time, I could count on receiving the call.

_____ 18. If X couldn't get together with me as we planned, I would believe his/her excuse that something important had come up.

_____ 19. If X promised to do me a favor, he/she would follow through.

_____ 20. If X were going to give me a ride somewhere and didn't arrive on time, I would guess there was a good reason for the delay.

_____ 21. If we decided to meet somewhere for lunch, I would be certain he/she would be there.

ITEMS FOR WOMEN

_____ 1. If I were injured or hurt, I could depend on X to do what was best for me.

_____ 2. If X borrowed something of value and returned it broken, X would offer to pay for the repairs.

_____ 3. If my alarm clock was broken and I asked X to call me at a certain time, I could count on receiving the call.

_____ 4. If X agreed to feed my pet while I was away, I wouldn't worry about the kind of care it would receive.

_____ 5. If X promised to do me a favor, he/she would follow through.

_____ 6. If X were going to give me a ride somewhere and didn't arrive on time, I would guess there was a good reason for the delay.

_____ 7. I would be willing to lend X almost any amount of money because he/she would pay me back as soon as he/she could.

_____ 8. If X couldn't get together with me as we had planned, I would believe his/her excuse that something important had come up.

_____ 9. I could talk freely to X and know that he/she would want to listen.

_____10. X would never intentionally misrepresent my point of view to others.

_____11. If X knew what kinds of things hurt my feelings, I would never worry that he/she would use them against me, even if our relationship changed.

_____12. I would be able to confide in X and know that he/she would not discuss my concerns with others.

_____13. I could expect X to tell me the truth.

Reprinted with permission of Dr. Walter C. Swap. For more information see: C. Johnson-George, and W. C. Swap (1982). "Measurement of Specific Interpersonal Trust: Construction and Validation of a Scale to Assess Truth in a Specific Other." *Journal of Personality and Social Psychology,* 43, 306–17.

SCORING

The only items that must be reversed (9 = 1, 8 = 2, 7 = 3, etc.) are 1 and 9 on the Male form of the test. For men, after you have reversed your score for these items, you can find scores on three subscales. The first is Overall Trust (OT) and is comprised of items 1 through 9; the second is Emotional Trust (ET) and includes items 10 through 16; and the third is Reliableness (Re), which includes items 17 through 21. Women can find scores on two subscales: Reliableness (Re), which consists of items 1 through 7, and Emotional Trust (ET), which is comprised of items 8 through 13.

NORMS

	SCORES				PERCENTILE
Men				Women	
OT	ET	Re	Re	ET	
81	63	45	63	54	85
77	57	41	61	53	70
69	50	36	56	49	50
61	43	31	51	45	30
54	37	26	46	41	15

About the Specific Interpersonal Trust Scale

The capacity to trust is crucial to our survival in human society. Without trust, we would not be willing to participate in even mundane interactions such as buying food at the grocery store, forming a car pool with neighbors, or visiting a physician. We have to believe that the food we buy at the store is safe, that our neighbors will pick us up on their day to drive, and that our physician will treat us in a way that will improve our health, not harm it. In even the most basic of social interactions, we are exposing our vulnerabilities, and without a willingness to trust those we interact with, we would all be living in solitary log cabins and growing our own food. Our existence would be both spartan and harsh, and our time on this earth would be much shorter than we can expect under our present way of life.

Research psychologists became interested in the capacity for trust in the 1970s, and a number of tests were developed to measure this quality. Their research showed that people with a high ability to trust seemed to have a number of other desirable qualities. They were more independent and trustworthy themselves, and as you might expect, they were more willing to seek out help from others.

Cynthia Johnson-George and Walter Swap, the authors of the Specific Interpersonal Trust Scale, raised some important questions about this early research that suggested that myriad benefits accompanied the capacity to trust others. First, they argued that a blind trust in other people may be naive and can be potentially dangerous. A healthy dose of skepticism when buying a used car will serve most people well, and a blanket refusal to trust hitchhiking strangers could save one's life. Second, a healthy trust of others might be specific to certain situations. We might not trust our spouse to fix our car, for instance, and we might not trust our mechanic with our deep, dark secrets. The test in this section resulted from the authors' belief that we could learn more about an individual's capacity to trust by relating it to specific others and specific situations.

One of the most surprising things Johnson-George and Swap found while constructing their test was that men and women think about trust in very different ways—so different that it necessitated separate tests for the sexes. As the two tests reflect, women tend to think of trust in more specific ways than do men; hence, there is no Overall Trust subscale for women. Second, women are consistently more trusting than men and more willing to give people a second chance after they have shown they cannot be trusted. The authors did find, however, that both men and women distinguish reliableness from emotional trust, and this seems to make sense. We have all had friends to whom we could tell anything, but who could not be counted on to remember an important date.

If you had a score below the 30th percentile on only one of the dimensions of trust, but your other scores were above average, it may say something accurate about your relationship with the person you used as X. Perhaps this person really is reliable but cannot be trusted with a secret. You might find it useful to take the test again, using a different person as X. If you get a different pattern of results, your judgments may be an accurate reflection of the people in your life. But if you receive a low score on the same dimension of trust no matter who you use as X, it probably reflects problems you have in this area. In this case, you must ask yourself why you have so much trouble counting on others or in believing your confidences are safe with them.

If you received low scores on both dimensions of trust (for women) or all three dimensions (for men), it may indicate that you have a more general difficulty in trusting other people. Again, take the test a second time with a different X, but if you always receive very low scores, it probably does reflect your diminished capacity for trust. And your diminished capacity for trust is undoubtedly interfering with your ability to have satisfying relationships with others.

In my experience the most difficult issue for most people is regaining trust in another after we have had good reason to distrust that person. John, a navy man I knew several years ago, learned that his wife had been unfaithful to him while he was out to sea. He was both furious and crushed, but he could not bring himself to divorce her because he loved her so much. He came to see me because his distrust was making him miserable. His worry made it difficult for him to sleep on subsequent cruises, and when he would call his wife, their conversations invariably degenerated into angry inquisitions.

Trust is indeed fragile; it is difficult to regain once lost. But as John realized, learning to trust again can benefit everyone if the relationship is truly worth saving. John decided he had to leave the navy because he doubted he could ever feel comfortable being separated from his wife for months at a time. And he came to understand that asking his wife to move to a strange city where she had no family or friends made her vulnerable to the attentions of other men.

John also came to understand that his distrust would eventually destroy his marriage. His suspicions were not only making him miserable, but his wife's stomach would also be tied in knots if she arrived home a few minutes late, knowing what was to come. With much encouragement, John agreed to stop voicing his suspicions. Rather than questioning his wife about her activities when she arrived home, he gave her a big hug and offered to fix her a glass of iced tea.

The first few months were difficult for John, and he had more than one slip. But his wife responded to his attempts to be more affectionate and trusting, and their relationship gradually grew stronger. After three years, John had occasional moments when he felt the pain of his wife's infidelity, but he also had developed a clear sense of confidence that it would never happen again. John learned that a relationship worth preserving demands a willingness to trust one's partner.

15
How Romantic Are You?

> ## THE ROMANTIC
> ## RELATIONSHIP SCALE

The following statements concern opinions and feelings that you may hold toward another person. With respect to the member of the opposite sex with whom you are most involved at the present time (designated as X), indicate the extent to which you agree or disagree with each statement by writing in the number that best expresses your opinion or feeling according to the key below:

1 = Strongly disagree

2 = Moderately disagree

3 = Slightly disagree

4 = Slightly agree

5 = Moderately agree

6 = Strongly agree

_____ 1. X's presence makes any activity more enjoyable.

_____ 2. X is close to my ideal as a person.

_____ 3. I am very lucky to be involved in a relationship with X.

_____ 4. I find myself wanting X when we're not together.

_____ 5. My relationship with X has given my life more direction and purpose.

_____ 6. I spend more time thinking about my career than I do about X.

_____ 7. I'd be extremely depressed for a long time if my relationship with X were to end.

_____ 8. If I couldn't have X, I'd easily find someone to replace X.

_____ 9. My relationship with X has made my life more worthwhile.

_____10. I don't really need X.

_____11. I want X.

_____12. I am very dependent upon X.

_____13. I feel very proud to know X.

_____14. I want X to confide mostly in me.

_____15. I spend a great deal of time thinking about X.

_____16. I want X to tell me "I love you."

_____17. I feel very secure in my relationship with X.

_____18. X is a rather mysterious person.

_____19. I often wonder how much X really cares for me.

_____20. Sometimes, I wish I didn't care so much for X.

_____21. I worry that X doesn't care as much for me as I do for X.

_____22. I have great difficulty trying to figure out X.

_____23. I have imagined conversations I would have with X.

_____24. I try to plan out what I want to say before talking to X.

_____25. X pays enough attention to me.

_____26. I feel uneasy if X is making friends with someone of the opposite sex.

_____27. I need X more than X needs me.

_____28. X has been the cause of some of my worst depressions.

_____29. My relationship with X is stable and quietly satisfying.

_____30. There is little conflict between X and myself.

_____31. I worry about losing X's affection.

Reprinted with permission of Dr. Ellen Berscheid. For more information see: E. Berscheid, M. Attridge, and S. Sprecher (1998). "Dependency and Insecurity in Romantic Relationships: Development and Validation of Two Companion Scales." *Personal Relationships*, 5, 31–58.

SCORING

The first step is to reverse the score (1 = 6, 2 = 5, 3 = 4, 4 = 3, 5 = 2, and 6 = 1) for the following items: 6, 8, 10, 17, 25, 29, and 30. Next, you can find your score on two subscales. The first 16 items comprise the Romantic Dependency subscale and items 17 to 31 comprise the Romantic Insecurity subscale.

NORMS

SCORE		PERCENTILE
Dependency	*Insecurity*	
91	57	85
81	48	70
71	38	50
61	28	30
51	17	15

About the Romantic Relationship Scale

Research psychologists have been trying to unlock the mysteries of romantic love for the past three decades. To facilitate their quest, they have developed dozens, perhaps hundreds of tests to measure every single aspect of romantic love you could ever think of, and many that you would never think of. One of the most prolific of these researchers, Ellen Berscheid, along with her colleagues Mark Attridge and Susan Sprecher, developed this Romantic Relationship Scale to measure two basic components of romantic love: dependency and insecurity. Berscheid agreed with other love researchers that dependency was an almost essential element of romantic love, but she was not certain about the role of insecurity. While it seems possible that one could be dependent on a partner while not feeling insecure about the relationship, it does make sense that one would worry about a relationship that one was dependent upon for happiness. The Romantic Relationship Scale has been used in a number of studies to learn more about how this all works. Let us take a look at what we have learned.

First, people who are in love score high on the Dependency subscale. This probably comes as a surprise to no one. After all, the very nature of romantic love makes us enjoy activities more if we share them with a loved one, and our feelings of love motivate us to spend as much time as possible with our partner. When we are in love we believe our very existence is dependent upon being with that special person.

It is important to understand that this is a subjective dependence specific to the love relationship and not a more general dependence that affects all relationships. Highly independent people who are generally quite self-sufficient still feel that their happiness depends on their partner when they are in love. These people may be seen by others as quite independent, and indeed, if their relationship goes badly, they may be able to move on with little difficulty. But nonetheless, when in the throes of love, they feel a longing for, a dependence on their partner.

Your score on the dependency scale does reflect the status of your relationship. Married people score higher on this scale than do couples who are dating exclusively, who in turn score higher than dating couples who also date other people. Also, high scores on the Dependency subscale are associated with high levels of commitment to, and greater satisfaction with the relationship. People who score high on this scale are generally happy with their partner and plan to stay in the relationship.

Insecurity seems to be a little more complicated. Berscheid and her colleagues found that, overall, there was no relationship between dependency and insecurity. This means that while some highly dependent people were insecure about their partner, other dependent people were quite secure.

It seems that insecurity is related to a number of factors, including the status of the relationship, the partner's feelings about the relationship, and the individual's general feelings about relationships. With respect to the status of the relationship, as you might expect, married couples were the most secure, while people in nonexclusive dating relationships were the least secure. Also, people who are in love with their partner and people who are not in love with their dating partner are more secure than people who are "not sure" if they are in love. It appears that as relationships progress toward exclusivity and commitment, the partners are likely to feel more secure about each other. But there is more.

Feeling secure also depends on your partner's feelings about the relationship. To learn if insecurity was related to actual relationship experiences, Berscheid and her colleagues looked at a variety of the test scores of those whose partners were feeling insecure about the relationship. To no one's surprise, they found that these partners had low levels of commitment to the relationship and believed there were better alternatives just waiting to be found. In other words, if you received a high score on the Insecurity subscale, it may be because you know or sense that your partner does not feel as strongly about your relationship as you do. Unfortunately, you may very well have good reason to feel insecure.

Finally, Berscheid found evidence that people with high scores on the Insecurity subscale may be generally insecure about their relationships. This notion is related to what psychologists call

attachment theory. Briefly, this idea suggests that our adult relationships are influenced by the nature of the attachment bond
we had with our parents. If we never felt secure in the love of our
parents, we are likely to have difficulty feeling secure in relationships as adults. Berscheid found that people with high scores on
the Insecurity subscale tended to have either an Insecure-Avoidant
or an Insecure-Anxious attachment style. The important point is
that these people are prone to experiencing feelings of insecurity in most of their romantic relationships.

To summarize, if you did receive a high score on the Insecurity
subscale, it could mean one of three things. First, it may simply
be that you are in a relatively new relationship and you want it to
progress to a more exclusive stage. At this stage, insecurity is a
perfectly normal feeling, one that virtually everyone has when
they find someone they are quite interested in but are unsure if
their feelings are reciprocated.

Second, your feelings of insecurity may reflect a sense of your
partner's doubts about the relationship. There is no easy cure for
this, but you can know if this is the case by talking openly with
your partner. Remember, the truth always will serve you best, so
ask about your partner's feelings without tears, threats, or re-
criminations—which would not improve the chances of improving your relationship in any case.

The third possibility is that your insecurity reflects experiences you had earlier in life. This is especially likely to be the case
if you have felt insecure in many, if not most, of your romantic relationships. If you see yourself in this possibility, you may come to
feel more confident about your relationship by discussing your
feelings with your partner. You may also find it useful to discuss
your concerns with a good therapist. Good luck.

16
How Guilty Are You about Sex?

```
┌─────────────────────────────────┐
│       THE REVISED MOSHER        │
│       GUILT INVENTORY           │
└─────────────────────────────────┘
```

This inventory consists of 50 items arranged in pairs of responses written by college students in response to sentence completion stems such as "When I have sexual dreams..." You are to respond to each item as honestly as you can by rating your response on a 7-point scale from 0, which means *not at all true of (for) me*, to 6, which means *extremely true of (for) me*. The items are arranged in pairs of two to permit you to compare the intensity of a *trueness* for you. This limited comparison is often useful, since people frequently agree with only one item in a pair. In some instances, it may be the case that both items or neither item is true for you, but you will usually be able to distinguish between items in a pair by using different ratings from the 7-point range for each item.

Rate each of the 50 items from 0 to 6 as you keep in mind the value of comparing items within pairs. Please do not omit any items.

"Dirty" jokes in mixed company . . .

_____ 1. do not bother me.

_____ 2. are something that make me very uncomfortable.

Masturbation . . .

_____ 3. is wrong and will ruin you.

_____ 4. helps one feel eased and relaxed.

Sex relations before marriage . . .

_____ 5. should be permitted.

_____ 6. are wrong and immoral.

Sex relations before marriage . . .

_____ 7. ruin many a happy couple.

_____ 8. are good in my opinion.

Unusual sex practices . . .

_____ 9. might be interesting.

_____10. don't interest me.

When I have sexual dreams . . .

_____11. I sometimes wake up feeling excited.

_____12. I try to forget them.

"Dirty" jokes in mixed company . . .

_____13. are in bad taste.

_____14. can be funny depending on the company.

Petting . . .

_____15. I am sorry to say is becoming an accepted practice.

_____16. is an expression of affection that is satisfying.

Unusual sex practices . . .

_____17. are not so unusual.

_____18. don't interest me.

Sex . . .

_____19. is good and enjoyable.

_____20. should be saved for wedlock and childbearing.

"Dirty" jokes . . .

_____21. are coarse to say the least.

_____22. are lots of fun.

When I have sexual desires . . .

_____23. I enjoy it like all healthy human beings.

_____24. I fight them for I must have complete control of my body.

Unusual sex practices . . .

_____25. are unwise and lead only to trouble.

_____26. are all in how you look at it.

Unusual sex practices . . .

_____27. are okay as long as they're heterosexual.

_____28. usually aren't pleasurable because you have preconceived feelings about their being wrong.

Sex relations before marriage . . .

_____29. in my opinion, should not be practiced.

_____30. are practiced too much to be wrong.

As a child, sex play . . .

_____31. is immature and ridiculous.

_____32. was indulged in.

Unusual sex practices . . .

_____33. are dangerous to one's health and mental condition.

_____34. are the business of those who carry them out and no one else's.

When I have sexual desires . . .

____35. I attempt to repress them.

____36. they are quite strong.

Petting . . .

____37. is not a good practice until after marriage.

____38. is justified with love.

Sex relations before marriage . . .

____39. help people adjust.

____40. should not be recommended.

Masturbation . . .

____41. is wrong and a sin.

____42. is a normal outlet for sexual desire.

Masturbation . . .

____43. is all right.

____44. is a form of self-destruction.

Unusual sex practices . . .

____45. are awful and unthinkable.

____46. are all right if both partners agree.

If I had sex relations, I would feel . . .

____47. all right, I think.

____48. I was being used, not loved.

Masturbation . . .

____49. is all right.

____50. should not be practiced.

SCORING

HOW GUILTY ARE YOU ABOUT SEX?139

Reprinted with permission of Dr. Donald L. Mosher. For more information see: D. L. Mosher (1998). "Revised Mosher Guilt Inventory." In C. M. Davis, W. L. Yarber, R. Bauserman, G. Schreer, and S. L. Davis (Eds.). *Handbook of Sexuality-Related Measures.* Sage: Thousand Oaks, 1998.

SCORING

You must reverse score the following items (0 = 6, 1 = 5, 2 = 4, 3 = 3, 4 = 2, 5 = 1, 6 = 0): 1, 4, 5, 8, 9, 11, 14, 16, 17, 19, 22, 23, 26, 27, 30, 32, 34, 36, 38, 39, 42, 43, 46, 47, and 49. After reversing these items add your scores together to find your total guilt scores. Higher scores indicate higher levels of guilt.

NORMS

SCORE	PERCENTILE
201	85
178	70
154	50
130	30
107	15

About the Revised Mosher Guilt Inventory

Nothing can interfere with our ability to experience pleasure in our sexual relationships more than guilt and anxiety. Mosher's test measuring guilt about sex is similar to one that I developed with my graduate student Kevin O'Grady to measure anxiety about sex. While guilt and anxiety may seem similar, they are theoretically different, and they have different effects on sexual behavior. By definition, guilty people worry about breaking their own moral rules; they feel bad if they engage in some sexual be-havior that they do not believe to be proper. Anxious people, on the other hand, are concerned about what others might think of them should they behave in a sexual manner. Kevin and I learned that they tend to go together; a number of people feel both guilty and anxious about their sexuality. But we also found that a number of people had high levels of guilt about sex but lit-tle anxiety, while others felt anxious but not guilty.

Stephanie, for instance, believed that it was appropriate for her to have a sexual relationship with her boyfriend, for whom she cared deeply. But she could not get past her strict religious upbringing, which left her with the vague feeling that she was do-ing something wrong when she was physically intimate with him. Although she became highly aroused during the preliminaries, something would "click off" during intercourse, making it im-possible for her to orgasm.

Paul believed that anything that two consenting adults did in private was perfectly okay, but his sexual anxiety made it very dif-ficult for him to initiate sexual relationships. He would worry that the young woman he was dating would think it was too soon for the first kiss, the first caress of the breast, and so on. Paul's anxiety was so intense that he would be convinced that his ad-vances would be rebuffed, even though an objective observer would see ample evidence that the young woman involved was enthusiastic about the prospect of greater physical intimacy.

While guilt and anxiety do go together for many people, they are conceptually different, and psychologists believe they are re-lated to different styles of parental discipline. Parents who prefer to explain to their children why their behavior was wrong, who are likely to tell their children to "go to your room and think about what you did" are likely to instill guilt. Stephanie heard many such messages as part of her religious training as a child and from her mother, who never failed to point out "shameful" behavior in Stephanie's friends and acquaintances. Paul's par-ents were quite different. They never talked to him about what was acceptable, they simply offered swift but silent corporal punishment when they discovered him doing something they did not approve of. Paul still remembers the sting of his mother's slap when she discovered him reading a *Playboy* magazine.

Despite these differences between guilt and sex, the overall effects are similar. Both guilty and anxious people tend to have restricted sexual experiences, they do not enjoy their sexual experiences as fully as they might, and perhaps most important, they are not as likely to behave in a sexually responsible way. Let us say a little about this last point first. People who feel guilty or anxious about their sexuality have fewer experiences than do their conflict-free peers, but they do explore their sexuality in their own tentative way. However, because they find it difficult to acknowledge their sexuality, they do not take the requisite precautions for safe, responsible sex. Sexually conflicted adolescent girls wait an average of three months after becoming sexually active before they begin to use contraceptives. Their male counterparts find it extremely difficult to visit their local pharmacy to buy the necessary supplies for safe sex. And most astounding of all, many young couples do not even discuss the issues of contraception or disease prevention prior to their sexual encounters. It may be difficult for young men and women who are conflicted about their sexuality to participate in it, but it is even harder for them to talk about it.

If you received a high score on the Revised Mosher Guilt Inventory, there is good news. Except for extreme cases, most anxious and guilty people do feel more comfortable with their sexuality over time and with experience. Stephanie began to orgasm regularly eight months into her relationship. She has had two serious relationships since that first one, and while she reported some initial discomfort in both, she adjusted quickly and thoroughly enjoyed her sexual experiences. She has retained much of her parents' early moral training and would never have sex with a man that she did not love, but she also has come to believe there is nothing wrong with sex between two people who care about each other if it brings so much joy. Paul has adapted to his anxiety by developing his own style. Rather than expressing his interest in women by making physical advances, he shares his feelings verbally. When he believes the time is right, he tells the woman he is dating how much he likes her and how attractive he finds her. If the woman shares his feelings, he feels sufficient confidence to make the traditional physical advances, albeit more tentatively than many men would.

Stephanie and Paul are typical, and their stories make, I believe, an important point. Both continue to be influenced by their parents' views on sex, but they do not see this as necessarily bad. Stephanie feels pity and some disdain for her friends who have casual sexual experiences. She believes such encounters are bad for her friends' self-esteem as well as dangerous to their health. And Paul would never want to be known as a womanizer. He has noticed that his male friends, who have a knack for finding one-night stands, seem to spend much of their time with their buddies bragging about their exploits rather than spending it with a woman they like. While Paul does have wistful moments when he wonders what it would be like to have sex with lots of different woman, he does strongly prefer his style of one, caring relationship at a time. Both Stephanie and Paul would argue that the remnants of guilt and anxiety that they feel serve to make them better people.

If your sexual guilt or anxiety is so intense that you find it impossible to get your sex life off the ground, you can make progress if you have a supportive partner. Share your fears and concerns with him or her, let this person know you will have to go slowly, and that you will need lots of encouragement and support. There are many self-help books that will give you useful ideas about specific steps you can try for your particular situation. These techniques really do work. There is every reason to believe that you can learn to enjoy your sexuality.

If you have avoided relationships because you do not want anyone to learn about your conflicts, you might want to rethink your position. Movies and television would have us believe that most everyone is sexually confident and competent, but the reality is that most people have their share of insecurities. If you form a relationship based on trust and caring, the odds are excellent that you may be able to help your partner as well as receive help and support from him or her. As always, if you find the prospect of changing on your own too daunting, please seek professional help. Life is too short to miss out on the joy that comes from connecting sexually with the right person.

SECTION III
IN SEARCH OF SELF-GROWTH

17

How Good Are You at Turning Your Bad Moods Around?

THE NEGATIVE MOOD REGULATION SCALE

This is a questionnaire to find out what people believe they can do about upsetting emotions or feelings. Please answer each statement by giving as true a picture of your own beliefs as possible. Of course, there are no right or wrong answers. Remember, the questionnaire is about what you *believe* you can do, not about what you actually or usually do. Be sure to read each item carefully and show your beliefs using the guidelines below:

> 1 = Strongly disagree
> 2 = Mildly disagree
> 3 = Agree and disagree equally
> 4 = Mildly agree
> 5 = Strongly agree

_____ 1. I can usually find a way to cheer myself up.

_____ 2. I can do something to feel better.

_____ 3. Wallowing in it is all I can do.

_____ 4. I'll feel okay if I think about more pleasant times.

_____ 5. Being with other people will be a drag.

_____ 6. I can feel better by treating myself to something I like.

_____ 7. I'll feel better when I understand why I feel bad.

_____ 8. I won't be able to get myself to do anything about it.

_____ 9. I won't feel much better by trying to find some good in the situation.

_____ 10. It won't be long before I can calm myself down.

_____ 11. It will be hard to find someone who really understands.

_____ 12. Telling myself it will pass will help me calm down.

_____ 13. Doing something nice for someone else will cheer me up.

_____ 14. I'll end up feeling really depressed.

_____ 15. Planning how I'll deal with things will help.

_____ 16. I can forget about what's upsetting me pretty easily.

_____ 17. Catching up with my work will help me calm down.

_____ 18. The advice friends give me won't help me feel better.

_____ 19. I won't be able to enjoy the things I usually enjoy.

_____ 20. I can find a way to relax.

_____ 21. Trying to work the problem out in my head will only make it seem worse.

_____ 22. Seeing a movie won't help me feel better.

_____ 23. Going out to dinner with friends will help.

_____ 24. I'll be upset for a long time.

_____ 25. I won't be able to put it out of my mind.

_____ 26. I can feel better by doing something creative.

_____ 27. I'll start to feel really down about myself.

_____ 28. Thinking that things will eventually be better won't help me feel any better.

_____ 29. I can find some humor in the situation and feel better.

_____ 30. If I'm with a group of people, I'll feel "alone in a crowd."

Reprinted with permission of Dr. Salvatore J. Catanzaro. For more information see: S. J. Catanzaro, and J. Mearns (1990). "Measuring Generalized Expectancies for Negative Mood Regulation: Initial Scale Development and Implications." *Journal of Personality Assessment,* 54, 546–63.

SCORING

The first step is to reverse the score (5 = 1, 4 = 2, 3 = 3, 2 = 4, and 1 = 5) for the following items: 3, 5, 8, 9, 11, 14, 18, 19, 21, 22, 24, 25, 27, 28, and 30. Then add your responses for your total score.

NORMS

SCORE	PERCENTILE
116	85
108	70
100	50
92	30
84	15

About the Negative Mood Regulation Scale

Everyone has days when they feel at least somewhat over-whelmed by stress or depression. It's just part of life. Since these bad days are inevitable, it is crucial to be able to get past them and move on to better times. If you received a high score on this test, you are probably one of those people who are quite good at putting bad times behind you and moving on to better things. If you received a low score, you could reduce the times you feel bad by learning more effective coping strategies. Salvatore Catanzaro and Jack Mearns developed this test to learn more about people who seem to be naturals when it comes to coping with negative moods, the sort of people who have a knack for helping themselves feel better when they experience one of those dark, frightening days.

The ability to regulate negative moods seems to begin early in life. Children as young as age six begin to cope differently with bad feelings. Some young children have clear beliefs about what they can do to get past feelings of sadness, fear, or anger, while others feel relatively helpless in the face of these negative emotions. At the other end of the life cycle, Catanzaro found that elderly women who coped well with the stress of caring for someone with Alzheimer's disease scored higher on this test. Catanzaro, Mearns, and a number of other researchers have collected an impressive body of evidence that shows that throughout life, people who receive high scores on this test do cope more effectively with stress.

Catanzaro and Mearns have conducted a number of studies to better understand the difference between people who are good at regulating their negative moods and those who are not. They have been able to rule out several explanations. There do not appear to be any differences in personality or temperament between the two groups, nor is it the case that high scorers simply experience fewer stressful events. The critical difference appears to be that high scorers have a firm belief that they can influence their moods, while low scorers feel relatively helpless when they experience distressing emotions. So, it would do little good to make specific suggestions to those who cannot turn their negative emotions around. Recommending that a depressed or anxious person visit a friend or see a movie would probably have little effect. They would claim that it "wouldn't do any good." They simply do not believe there is anything they can do about their bad feelings.

Catanzaro and Mearns did not recommend any specific form of therapy for low scorers, but they did state that the therapist must help clients come to believe that their actions can disrupt their negative emotions, that they do not have to be passive victims of either circumstances or their moods. One particular approach that might be especially helpful for low scorers is called solution-focused therapy. Sandy, a young mother of two preschool children, sought help for her chronic feelings of tension and anxiety. She worked full time, so she had a hectic schedule— which she blamed for her negative moods. She had little hope that therapy would make any real difference. She simply wanted to survive until her children were a little older and a little more self-sufficient.

One of the first tasks that Sandy's therapist gave her was to keep records of the degree of stress she felt each day. Sandy objected at first. She did not see the point, since she felt highly stressed every workday, and only somewhat less stressed on the weekends. But she complied and at her second session showed her therapist her chart indicating that on Tuesday she felt better than she had the other workdays. The first question her therapist asked was, "What did you do different on Tuesday?"

Sandy replied in a somewhat annoyed voice, "Nothing, it was just a less hectic day." Sandy was not ready to acknowledge even the possibility that it was her actions that may have made the difference.

After several more weeks of charting her stress level, Sandy eventually came to see a pattern. She felt more relaxed on those days when she planned a simple meal so she could spend more fun time with the children. As therapy progressed, Sandy came to realize that she did have solutions available to her, she simply had not recognized them. She talked with her therapist about other strategies she might use to make her life less hectic, and after eight sessions she felt much better. More important, she had developed a sense of confidence that she did have the ability to make her life different, that she could take steps to help herself feel more relaxed.

Sandy's experience reflects a theme that runs throughout

much of psychotherapy and one that we have touched on in several chapters in this book, namely, that people feel better when they have a sense that they are in control of their lives rather than the hapless victim of circumstances. I believe that helping people gain this sense of control is the most important component of solution-focused therapy. The solution itself does not matter nearly as much as the firm belief that there are available solutions to be found. So it does not matter if Sandy reduces her negative emotions by going to a movie, visiting with friends, or structuring her time so she can read stories to her children. The key is that she came to believe that she could find solutions to overcome her negative emotions.

If you received a low score on this test, the best place to start is by identifying the solutions that work best for you. Keep a chart of your negative emotions. Some days will be better than others, and you have to identify what you did differently on your good days. Yes, it is true that some people are more fortunate than others, but none of us are helpless about doing something about our circumstances. As long as you believe you can make a difference, you will. All you have to do is identify solutions that work for you.

18
How Effective a Person Are You?

```
THE SELF-EFFICACY
       SCALE
```

The following statements describe people's feelings and reactions to various situations. Please read each statement carefully and describe the extent to which you agree with each statement, using a 14-point scale where 1 indicates "Strongly Disagree" and 14 indicates "Strongly Agree."

_____ 1. When I make plans, I am certain I can make them work.

_____ 2. One of my problems is that I cannot get down to work when I should.

_____ 3. If I can't do a job the first time, I keep trying until I can.

_____ 4. When I set important goals for myself, I rarely achieve them.

_____ 5. I give up on things before completing them.

_____ 6. I avoid facing difficulties.

_____ 7. If something looks too complicated, I will not even bother to try it.

_____ 8. When I have something unpleasant to do, I stick to it until I finish it.

_____ 9. When I decide to do something, I go right to work on it.

_____10. When trying to learn something new, I soon give up if I am not initially successful.

_____11. When unexpected problems occur, I don't handle them well.

_____12. I avoid trying to learn new things when they look too difficult for me.

_____13. Failure just makes me try harder.

_____14. I feel insecure about my ability to do things.

_____15. I am a self-reliant person.

_____16. I give up easily.

_____17. I do not seem capable of dealing with most problems that come up in life.

_____18. It is difficult for me to make new friends.

_____19. If I see someone I would like to meet, I go to that person instead of waiting for him or her to come to me.

_____20. If I meet someone interesting who is hard to make friends with, I'll soon stop trying to make friends with that person.

_____21. When I'm trying to become friends with someone who seems uninterested at first, I don't give up easily.

_____22. I do not handle myself well in social gatherings.

_____23. I have acquired my friends through my personal abilities at making friends.

Reprinted with permission of Dr. James E. Maddux of George Mason University. For more information see: M. Sherer, J. E. Maddux, B. Mercandante, S. Prentice-Dunn, B. Jacobs, and R. W. Rogers (1982). "The Self-Efficacy Scale: Construction and Validation." *Psychological Reports*, 51, 663–71.

SCORING

The first step is to reverse the score (14 = 1, 13 = 2, 12 = 3, etc.) for the following items: 2, 4, 5, 6, 7, 10, 11, 12, 14, 16, 17, 18, 20, and 22. After completing this step, you can find your scores on two subscales: the General Self-Efficacy subscale consists of items 1 through 17, and the Specific Self-Efficacy subscale is comprised of items 18 through 23.

NORMS

GENERAL SELF-EFFICACY	SPECIFIC SELF-EFFICACY	PERCENTILE
199	70	85
186	64	70
172	58	50
158	52	30
145	46	15

About the Self-Efficacy Scale

If you had a high score on this test, you probably feel confident about your ability to make changes in your life and to accomplish your goals. This sense of confidence is not an illusion, you are indeed more likely to achieve success in your personal life, and your educational and vocational endeavors than those who obtained low scores on this test. Stanford psychologist Albert Bandura, one of the most respected researchers in the country, has called self-efficacy one of the most powerful determinants of behavioral change because it causes people to take that first step toward their goal, it motivates them to make a concerted effort, and it gives them the strength to persist in the face of adversity.

This may make it seem that self-efficacy is only relevant to the highly functioning, go-getters of the world, but a sense of self-efficacy is important to everyone, regardless of whether they head a major corporation or are struggling in psychotherapy to overcome a personal problem. Indeed, Bandura has found that a sense of self-efficacy does predict a good outcome for clients in psychotherapy. The Self-Efficacy Scale you just completed was constructed by Mark Sherer and James Maddux to be used by therapists to gauge the progress of treatment. As part of their work, they found that among veterans receiving treatment for alcoholism, those with a sense of self-efficacy had a more successful job history, had more education, and had achieved a higher military rank than their low-scoring peers. Self-efficacy is important to everyone, and those without it can improve their lot in life by working to develop this important trait.

A sense of self-efficacy develops as one has successful experiences and (this is a critical *and*) takes credit for making those successes happen. Success alone does not guarantee self-efficacy. One has to believe that his or her efforts were responsible for the success. I knew two graduate students whose experiences illustrate this point vividly. The first, John, was a brilliant student and school always came easily to him. He was selected as his college's outstanding physics student and was accepted to one of the top graduate programs in the country for his doctoral work. All of his instructors were confident he would have a distinguished career. Ken, one of John's graduate school classmates, was also selected as his department's outstanding major as an undergraduate, but he had to work harder for his success. He was extremely bright, but the upper-level physics and math classes did not come as easily to him as they did to John, and Ken spent countless evenings burning the midnight oil. During their second year of graduate school, John finally reached the point where he had difficulty grasping certain complex material, and he panicked. This had never happened to him and he did not know what to do. Ken, on the other hand, had learned several years earlier that he would have to struggle for some time before that sense of finally understanding the material would come over him. More than once he could be found at his desk working problems as the sun rose. He pestered his professors with questions, and sure enough, he eventually reached the point where he "got it." John never did. After floundering for four years, he left the program with a master's degree and accepted a position teaching at a junior college. There is nothing wrong with that, of course, but John felt the sting of failure for years. Ken, on the other hand, earned his Ph.D. in four years and went on to have a distinguished academic and research career. He still recognizes his limitations; it is not unusual for him to ask one of his gifted graduate students to help him with the math involved in his work. But no one would bet against him if he ever said he could solve a problem.

John's problem was that he had always explained his successes as resulting from his gifted intelligence. When this failed him, he had nothing to fall back on. Other successful people may reach their limits sooner than necessary because they explain their successes in terms of luck, or good fortune. You do not have to approve of Donald Trump to admire what he has done with his comparatively modest inheritance from his father. There have been countless other people who began with more resources and did much less with them. It was, I'm sure, Trump's unwavering sense of self-efficacy that allowed him to turn a few apartment buildings into one of the world's greatest real estate empires. If you received a low score on this test, the first place to start is to take more credit for your successes. Perhaps you are truly lucky, perhaps you are bright, perhaps your successes were minor. But even if all of this were true, your success still depended on your effort. Undergraduate work came easily to John, but he still had to study the material for the exams, and he still had to work hard to complete his honors thesis. His career would have turned out much different if he had told himself, "I'm go-ing to have to step up my efforts," rather than, "I've reached my intellectual limit," during his second year of graduate school.

I know that some people with low scores on this test will com-plain, "What you wrote doesn't apply to me because I haven't had any success experiences." My response would be a simple, "You're wrong." If you are reading these words, you have been successful in mastering a critical skill. If you could calculate your score on the test, you have mastered a second critical skill. You have had success experiences, so that is not the problem. My guess is that your problem lies in setting appropriate goals.

I have seen countless students over the years who have a seri-ous goal-setting problem. They begin their freshman year with dreams of becoming a physician, lawyer, research scientist, and the like, but then halfway through their first semester, they begin to miss class because they partied too much the night before. It is a noble goal to want to be a doctor, lawyer, or research scien-tist, but it is critical to have short-term goals that allow you to move steadily toward your long-term goals. If you believe you have failed to reach your goals, make a list of the steps you would have to take to get there and begin with the very first step on that list. The first step might be to take one course at the local com-munity college. Perhaps it might be to begin saving $10 per week so you can buy the equipment you need to start your own busi-ness. The key is to set small goals that are within your reach and to give yourself credit for reaching them. As the cliché suggests, nothing breeds success like success. Once you get started, there will be no stopping you.

19
How Hardy Are You?

> ## THE HARDINESS
> ## SCALE

Below are statements about life that people often feel differently about. Indicate a number to show how you feel about each one. Read the items carefully, and indicate how much you think each one is true in general. There are no right or wrong answers.

3 = Completely true
2 = Quite true
1 = A little true
0 = Not at all true

_____ 1. Most of my life gets spent doing things that are worthwhile.

_____ 2. Planning ahead can help avoid most future problems.

_____ 3. Trying hard doesn't pay, since things still don't turn out right.

_____ 4. No matter how hard I try, my efforts usually accomplish nothing.

_____ 5. I don't like to make changes in my everyday schedule.

_____ 6. The "tried and true" ways are always best.

_____ 7. Working hard doesn't matter, since only the bosses profit by it.

_____ 8. By working hard you can always achieve your goals.

_____ 9. Most working people are simply manipulated by their bosses.

_____10. Most of what happens in life is just meant to be.

_____11. It's usually impossible for me to change things at work.

_____12. New laws should never hurt a person's paycheck.

_____13. When I make plans, I'm certain I can make them work.

_____14. It's very hard for me to change a friend's mind about something.

_____15. It's exciting to learn something about myself.

_____16. People who never change their minds usually have good judgment.

_____17. I really look forward to my work.

_____18. Politicians run our lives.

_____19. If I'm working on a difficult task, I know when to seek help.

_____20. I won't answer a question until I'm really sure I understand it.

_____21. I like a lot of variety in my work.

_____22. Most of the time, people listen carefully to what I say.

_____23. Daydreams are more exciting than reality for me.

_____24. Thinking of yourself as a free person just leads to frustration.

_____25. Trying your best at work really pays off in the end.

_____26. My mistakes are usually very difficult to correct.

_____27. It bothers me when my daily routine gets interrupted.

_____28. It's best to handle most problems by just not thinking of them.

_____29. Most good athletes and leaders are born, not made.

_____30. I often wake up eager to take up my life wherever it left off.

_____31. Lots of times, I don't really know my own mind.

_____32. I respect rules because they guide me.

_____33. I like it when things are uncertain or unpredictable.

_____34. I can't do much to prevent it if someone wants to harm me.

_____35. People who do their best should get full support from society.

_____36. Changes in routine are interesting to me.

_____37. People who believe in individuality are only kidding themselves.

_____38. I have no use for theories that are not closely tied to facts.

_____39. Most days, life is really interesting and exciting for me.

_____40. I want to be sure someone will take care of me when I'm old.

_____41. It's hard to imagine anyone getting excited about working.

_____42. What happens to me tomorrow depends on what I do today.

_____43. If someone gets angry at me, it's usually no fault of mine.

_____44. It's hard to believe people who say their work helps society.

_____45. Ordinary work is just too boring to be worth doing.

Reprinted with permission of Dr. Paul T. Bartone of the U.S. Naval Academy. For more information see: P. Bartone, R. J. Ursano, K. M. Wright, and L. H. Ingraham (1989). "The Impact of a Military Air Disaster on the Health of Assistance Workers." *Journal of Nervous and Mental Disease,* 177, 317–28.

SCORING

The score on the following items must be reversed (3 = 0, 2 = 1, 1 = 2, and 0 = 3): 3, 4, 5, 6, 7, 9, 10, 11, 12, 14, 16, 18, 20, 23, 24, 26, 29, 31, 32, 34, 35, 37, 38, 40, 41, 43, 44, and 45. After reversing these items, you can find your scores on three subscales. The items that appear on each subscale are as follows:

Commitment: 1, 7, 8, 9, 17, 18, 23, 24, 25, 31, 37, 39, 41, 44, and 45.
Control: 2, 3, 4, 10, 11, 13, 14, 19, 22, 26, 28, 29, 34, 42, and 43.
Challenge: 5, 6, 12, 15, 16, 20, 21, 27, 30, 32, 33, 35, 36, 38, and 40.
Finally, you can add these three scores together to obtain your Hardiness Scale score.

NORMS

SCORES				PERCENTILE
Commitment	Control	Challenge	Total	
56	49	43	148	85
53	47	41	141	70
50	45	39	134	50
47	43	37	127	30
44	41	35	120	15

About the Hardiness Scale

Some three decades ago, psychologist Deborah Khoshaba recognized that the breakup of AT&T represented a wonderful research opportunity. She reasoned that executives who worked for the company would experience a great deal of stress, since no one could know what the end result would be. She gave the executives a series of tests prior to the breakup and followed these people for some time after the restructuring was completed. Many of these people, as Khoshaba expected, had a difficult time during this transition period; some even experienced physical illnesses. Other executives seemed to thrive on this period of rapid change. They found that the transition period offered them fresh opportunities to prove their worth to their new company. Khoshaba concluded that what separated these two groups was their "hardiness." The executives who did well had what she called a hardy personality.

The hardy personality consists of three interrelated, yet distinct, components: commitment, control, and challenge. People with a strong sense of commitment are able to find ways of turning virtually any experience into something that they find both interesting and important. As opposed to low scorers on this scale, who are apt to become easily alienated, high scorers become actively involved with the experiences life presents them. People with high scores on the control scale believe that their efforts make a difference, that they can influence the course of events that confront them. Low scorers tend to remain passive. They see themselves as the victims of circumstances. Finally, people who score high on the challenge scale welcome new experiences because they offer the opportunity to increase their wisdom, to make them better people. Low scorers tend to shrink away from life's challenges. They seek refuge in easy comfort and a secure, predictable routine. Dr. Paul Bartone's test represents the "third generation" tool to measure hardiness.

Khoshaba's work inspired a flurry of research and it now appears that this measure of hardiness provides a good index of general mental health. Compared to low scorers, people with high total scores have less depression, anxiety, and suspiciousness of others, and fewer insecurities and health problems. Hardy personalities cope effectively with stressful events, and they tend to be assertive, independent people. Several studies have found that hardiness is associated with better performance in a variety of specific situations, ranging from basketball to officer training school.

If you had a low score on this test, be assured that it is possible to change. Salvatore Maddi, a colleague of Khoshaba, offers hardiness training to business executives, and he has found that his program leads to increased job satisfaction and reduced levels of depression and anxiety. Change is never easy, but with a sustained, consistent effort, it can be done. To illustrate how this process can work, let me describe the case of a former client, whom I will call Frank.

Frank had worked as a real estate agent for a number of years, but the uncertain income and irregular hours became increasingly onerous to him, so he accepted a position with a large development company to manage several apartment complexes. For the first six months, Frank liked his new job. The predictable paychecks and the free weekends were a welcome change. But over the following year, he began to worry that he had made a mistake. Much of his job required him to react to problems— emergency repairs or tenants who failed to pay their rent—and he missed the emotional high he experienced as an agent when he made a big sale. By the time he came to see me, he was both depressed and anxious. "I have to drag myself to work every morning, and every time the phone rings, my stomach knots up in anticipation of another crisis," he said.

Although Frank had allowed himself to be consumed with pessimism about his work, he had a number of strengths, so he was able to turn things around relatively quickly. The first change he had to make was to shift his focus from what he characterized as the "day-to-day drudgery" of his life to a long-term view. After some discussion, Frank decided to initiate a referral network for those tenants who were leaving to buy their own home. His company responded enthusiastically to his idea and agreed to split the commissions with him. Once Frank was able to view his tenants as potential clients, his attitude toward them did a complete turnaround. He welcomed calls about the hot water heater that was still not working because it gave him the opportunity to develop rapport with the caller. He even began to spend a half hour each day calling tenants to see if they had any problems that he could help them with. Frank's new attitude toward his tenants elicited a similar change in them. They began to view him as someone who could help them rather than another obstacle in the bureaucracy of the company. He still had to deal with the occasional angry tenant, but the general tone of his interactions become much more positive. He no longer dreaded going to work each morning.

To my mind, perhaps the key to the hardy personality is that these people eschew safe, secure, comfortable routines. They want to grow, to develop, to conquer new challenges. Frank was looking for a safe, comfortable routine when he took his new job, but he learned that such a routine could easily change into drudgery. Once Frank began to embrace new challenges, the other changes he needed to make were rather easy. If you received a low score on this test, I would recommend that you take a page from Frank's book and find new challenges for yourself. They do not have to be as dramatic as Frank's career change, even minor challenges can help you develop a fresher, more rewarding perspective. You might decide to become a more effective Little League coach—the kind of coach that children remember for the rest of their lives. Or you could find a new hobby to help revive your sense of pleasure in learning and to rediscover the satisfaction to be derived from mastering something new. Fresh challenges are to be found everywhere; all you need to do is look around you.

20
How Well Do You Cope with Traumatic Life Events?

Many times, people with a chronic illness or who have had traumatic experiences talk not only about the negative things, but also of the positive things that have happened to them as a result of their illness or experience. Below is a list of some of these positive things. On a scale of 0 (this did not happen to me) to 4 (I experienced a great deal of this) indicate the degree to which each occurred in your life as a result of your illness or traumatic experience.

_____ 1. I learned to look at things in a more positive way.

_____ 2. I learned that I am stronger than I thought I was.

_____ 3. I learned to be a more optimistic person.

_____ 4. I realized how much my family cares about me.

_____ 5. I learned to be more confident in myself.

_____ 6. I learned to approach life more calmly.

_____ 7. I have more compassion for others.

_____ 8. Now I know I can handle difficulties.

_____ 9. My relationship with my family became more important.

_____10. I learned to work through my problems and not give up.

_____11. I learned to find more meaning in life.

_____12. My faith in God increased.

_____13. My relationship with my family became more meaning-
ful.

_____14. My life now has more meaning and satisfaction.

_____15. I learned to appreciate the strength of others who have
difficult times.

_____16. My confidence in God increased.

_____17. I learned to live for today, because you never know
what will happen tomorrow.

_____18. Now I know that I can count on my friends in difficult
times.

_____19. I learned to deal better with uncertainty.

_____20. I learned to be more patient.

Reprinted with the permission of Dr. Anna F. Abraido-Lanza of the Columbia
School of Public Health. For more information see: A. F. Abraido-Lanza,
C. Guier, and R. M. Colon (1998). "Psychological Thriving Among Latinas with
Chronic Illness." *Journal of Social Issues,* 54, 405–24.

SCORING

To find your Thriving score, simply add together your responses
to the twenty items.

NORMS

Score	Percentile
74	85
67	70
60	50
53	30
46	15

About the Thriving Scale

We psychologists can be slow to catch on. While novelists, poets, and philosophers have been writing for centuries about the positive changes that people can experience as a result of adversity, we psychologists have only begun to explore this phenomenon. Over the years a number of mental health professionals have observed the personal growth their clients experienced as a result of trauma or illness, but it has only been during the last few years that research psychologists have tried to understand this process; a process that has come to be called either resiliency or thriving. The Thriving Scale, developed by Dr. Anna Abraido-Lanza and her colleagues at the Columbia School of Public Health, is one of the very first attempts to measure these positive changes. Their scale was developed to be used in their research with Latina women who suffered from arthritis, but it clearly has important implications for people who experience other diseases or hardship.

Perhaps one of the most interesting, and one of the most hopeful, discoveries these researchers have made is that so many people do experience positive changes when they struggle with adversity. Abraido-Lanza and her colleagues found, for instance, that fully 83 percent of the women they studied reported at least some positive changes as a result of their illness. And as you can tell from the norms for their scale, the typical woman in their research experienced quite dramatic positive changes (the average score for these women was 30 points out of a possible 40). This says something remarkable about the human spirit, that so many people can find meaning in their lives when their illness or trauma must seem so capricious.

We have learned that thriving or resiliency is not an all-or-none phenomenon. Abraido-Lanza only asked about positive changes on her scale, but had she asked about negative feelings, she undoubtedly would have found plenty of evidence for their existence. People can thrive and suffer at the same time. No matter how resilient people are, they are bound to retain many of the scars that bear witness to their trauma. Drs. Calhoun and Tedeschi, two prominent researchers in this field, described several people who experienced this duality. One, a middle-aged woman who suddenly lost her husband, talked with confidence about her growing sense of strength and her ability to live independently within a few months after her loss. Although it had no relevance to her trauma, she became actively involved with a support group for parents with gay children because she wanted to do something to help others who were in pain. On the other hand, her grief at her loss had not abated much, and she had developed doubts about her religious beliefs. Calhoun and Tedeschi wrote that while not all changes that may occur in response to a traumatic experience will be positive, the process of thriving does lead to a general increase in wisdom—an increased understanding of who we are, of the world, and of our place in it.

Another issue that researchers have addressed is whether thriving is an effortless process that occurs naturally or whether it requires a sustained endeavor. The answer, according to researchers Karen Saakvitne, Howard Tennen, and Glenn Affleck, seems to be "both." Some people experienced spontaneous positive changes. A young father, whose newborn daughter was acutely ill, reported: "Here she was, only a week old, and she was teaching us something: how to keep things in their proper perspective, how to understand what's important and what's not. I learned that everything is tentative, that you never learn what life is going to bring. I realized that I shouldn't waste any more time worrying about the little things." Other people these researchers interviewed talked about how they had to struggle to find meaning in their tragedies, about how much effort and how much time it took before they could find anything positive about their experience.

We have much to learn about the types of people who "thrive," but it does not appear to be the case that their ability to find wisdom in tragedy resulted from their unusual psychological strength. Before their illness or trauma, people who eventually thrived tended to rank only slightly higher than others in their self-esteem and their self-efficacy. Indeed, there are numerous examples of people who seemed to have significant problems before their trauma, and yet they found the resiliency within themselves that allowed them to thrive. Sandra, for instance, was in her late thirties and functioned at only a marginal level. She was completely dependent on her husband to make all decisions, both the important ones as well as the trivial. She was a stay-at-home mom who prided herself on her ability to keep a clean house, but she had difficulty coping with even the smallest problems her two teenaged children brought to her.

One day Sandra's husband called to tell her that he had fallen in love with another woman and that he would never be coming home again. Beyond the emotional devastation she felt, Sandra was extremely frightened. She had not held a job since high school, and she had dropped out of college after her junior year to marry. Her situation became even worse when she learned that her husband had quit his job and moved away from the area. She had enough money to last, at most, six weeks, and she did not have any idea what would happen to her after that.

Sandra did have six horrendous months, but she eventually began to grow stronger. She sold her house and moved into a modest apartment with her two girls. The proceeds from her house provided her with enough money to finish college and receive certification to teach high school. Five years after her devastating trauma, Sandra reported feeling happier than she had ever felt. She was an exceptionally effective teacher, and her students frequently came to her for advice about their personal problems. She was in a serious relationship with another divorced teacher, and while she dearly loved him, she was not certain whether she wanted to marry again. She had grown to love her independence and believed she had much more to discover about herself before taking a second chance. In short, Sandra thrived.

Abraido-Lanza did report that while women who eventually thrived were not much different from others before their illness, they were considerably different after three years. At that time, the thrivers were noticeably higher in self-esteem and self-efficacy than others, and they experienced significantly more positive emotions and significantly fewer negative emotions. Clearly, it is possible to experience personal growth as a result of illness or trauma.

There is an important lesson to be found in the cases described above. If you are among the many people who cannot find anything positive in life shortly after a traumatic experience, you should not give up. We know from this line of invaluable research that as long as people are persistent, and as long as they continue to struggle with the meaning of their experience, they are likely to find the wisdom that Calhoun and Tedeschi describe. For some fortunate few, this process may be both sudden and spontaneous, while for others it will require much effort and time. While the pain may never completely disappear, people can find a new sense of strength and a renewed appreciation for life as long as they are willing to make the effort.

21
How Empathic Are You?

THE EMPATHY
SCALE

The following statements describe feelings and reactions to a variety of situations. Using the scale below, indicate the degree to which you agree with each statement.

9 = Very strong agreement
8 = Strong agreement
7 = Moderate agreement
6 = Slight agreement
5 = Neither agree nor disagree
4 = Slight disagreement
3 = Moderate disagreement
2 = Strong disagreement
1 = Very strong disagreement

_____ 1. It makes me sad to see a lonely stranger in a group.

_____ 2. People make too much of the feelings and sensitivity of animals.

_____ 3. I often find public displays of affection annoying.

_____ 4. I am annoyed by unhappy people who are just sorry for themselves.

_____ 5. I become nervous if others around me seem to be nervous.

_____ 6. I find it silly for people to cry out of happiness.

_____ 7. I tend to get emotionally involved with a friend's problems.

_____ 8. Sometimes the words of a love song can move me deeply.

_____ 9. I tend to lose control when I am bringing bad news to people.

_____ 10. The people around me have a great influence on my moods.

_____ 11. Most foreigners I have met seemed cool and unemotional.

_____ 12. I would rather be a social worker than work in a job training center.

_____ 13. I don't get upset just because a friend is acting upset.

_____ 14. I like to watch people open presents.

_____ 15. Lonely people are probably unfriendly.

_____ 16. Seeing people cry upsets me.

_____ 17. Some songs make me happy.

_____ 18. I really get involved with the feelings of the characters in a novel.

_____ 19. I get very angry when I see someone being ill-treated.

_____ 20. I am able to remain calm even though those around me worry.

_____ 21. When a friend starts to talk about his problems, I try to steer the conversation to something else.

_____ 22. Another's laughter is not catching for me.

_____ 23. Sometimes at the movies I am amused by the amount of crying and sniffling around me.

_____ 24. I am able to make decisions without being influenced by people's feelings.

_____25. I cannot continue to feel okay if people around me are depressed.

_____26. It is hard for me to see how some things upset people so much.

_____27. I am very upset when I see an animal in pain.

_____28. Becoming involved in books or movies is a little silly.

_____29. It upsets me to see helpless old people.

_____30. I become more irritated than sympathetic when I see someone's tears.

_____31. I become very involved when I watch a movie.

_____32. I often find that I can remain cool in spite of the excitement around me.

_____33. Little children sometimes cry for no apparent reason.

Reprinted with permission of Dr. Norman Epstein. For more information see: A. Mehrabian, and N. Epstein (1972). "A Measure of Emotional Empathy." *Journal of Personality,* 40, 525–43.

SCORING

The first step is to reverse the score (9 = 1, 8 = 2, 7 = 3, 6 = 4, 5 = 5, 4 = 6, 3 = 7, 2 = 8, and 1 = 9) for the following items: 2, 3, 6, 11, 13, 15, 20, 21, 22, 23, 24, 28, 30, 32, and 33. Then add together your responses to the items.

NORMS

Score		Percentile
Men	Women	
210	230	85
199	220	70
188	209	50
177	198	30
166	188	15

About the Emotional Empathy Scale

Psychologists have been discussing the role of empathy in human relationships for decades, but it is interesting to note that various researchers have defined it in different ways. In one major camp theorists have conceptualized empathy as an intellectual or cognitive quality. According to this view, empathic people can imagine what it is like to be someone else, and this enables them to understand and predict that person's thoughts, feelings, and behaviors. Empathic people remain neutral and detached, and it is this very detachment that enables them to be objective in their predictions.

UCLA psychologists Albert Mehrabian and Norman Epstein, the authors of the test you just completed, took a very different view. They conceptualized empathy as a vicarious emotional response to the emotional reactions of others. Empathic people, argued Mehrabian and Epstein, are not only able to recognize the emotions of others, but they are also able to share the emotional experiences of others. Empathic people are the ones who shed tears of joy while vicariously sharing the triumphs of family, friends, and even strangers. Empathic people also feel the pain when they see others suffer.

While both conceptualizations of empathy have important implications for human behavior, I see Mehrabian and Epstein's emotional empathy as being the more critical to having a humane, civilized society. My conclusion, I'm sure, has been influenced by the year I spent working in a state prison while a graduate student. I met a number of extremely frightening men there who seemed to have almost no capacity for empathy. Their deficit was responsible, I believe, for their causing others unspeakable misery, and ultimately, for making themselves miserable. These were men who, as children, tortured animals for entertainment. As adults, it never bothered them to inflict pain, both emotional and physical, on others. They abused children, beat victims even though it served no purpose, and even killed people without feeling. Ours would be a truly barbaric world if none of us had any capacity for emotional empathy.

To support the validity of their test, Mehrabian and Epstein conducted two studies that are consistent with my experiences with some of the state prison inmates. First, they found that college students who scored high on their emotional empathy test were less willing than low scorers to "punish" fellow students for incorrect answers by administering electric shocks. (Actually, no shocks were delivered. The research participants only believed they were shocking their partner in the experiment.) In the second experiment, high scorers were more willing than low-scoring students to help a fellow student who was having trouble with a course. Clearly, emotional empathy serves to inhibit aggression and promote helping others. If you received a high score on this test, the odds are good that you are one of those people who make an important contribution to a civilized, humane society.

If you received a low score on the test, it does not mean that you are destined to inflict pain on others or to refuse lending a helping hand to those in need. Many of the low-scoring students in Mehrabian and Epstein's experiment administered a minimal level of electric shock and were quick to volunteer their help. It will be left to future researchers to find conclusive answers to this puzzle, but I believe it reflects the fact that both nature and nurture play a role in the development of empathy. Some children, I suspect, are born with a great capacity for empathy. They are quick to cry when they see either an animal or a playmate in pain. These children may lose their capacity to vicariously share others' experiences if their parents punish them for such displays. This may happen more often to boys than girls (a number of studies have found women to be more empathic than men), since their fathers are likely to punish them for "unmanly" displays of emotion. There are countless men who, as boys, hated to see animals suffer but eventually came to enjoy hunting to win their father's approval.

On the other side of the coin, I believe there are people who are born with little, and in extreme cases, no capacity to experience emotional empathy. I saw some of these extreme cases when I worked in the state prison. It was as if there was a hole in their soul. But other children who have little capacity for empathy become kind, helpful adults if they have the right parenting. Their kindness and helpfulness come from an intellectual understanding that this is the appropriate way to treat other people. And while these people may not have the same emotional reactions to others' experiences that highly empathic people do, their commitment to treat others with dignity and respect can be just as powerful.

There is some evidence that emotional empathy can be a double-edged sword. On the one hand, empathic people perform well in the helping professions, such as social work or teaching. Presumably, their ability to share their clients' or students' emotional reactions make them more sensitive to their needs and hence, more effective. This same sensitivity, however, makes them prone to early burnout. Over time, empathy can take a toll on people. If you did receive a score above the 85th percentile, it might be wise to give some thought to the emotional consequences of the career you select.

The authors of the Empathy Scale recognized that this trait consists of a number of interrelated, but distinct components. They placed the items on their test into seven different categories. Item 10, for instance, is in the category "Susceptibility to Emotional Contagion," item 15 is in the category "Appreciation of the Feelings of Unfamiliar and Distant Others," and item 14 falls under the category "Tendency to Be Moved by Others' Positive Emotional Experiences." This is important because I suspect it is likely that people may have intense reactions to situations that fall under some categories and very little reaction to others. I, to use a perfectly good example, hate to see animals suffer. I cannot enjoy even fishing because it means having to kill the fish. But on the other hand, I would have to strongly agree with item 26, "It is hard for me to see how some things upset people so much." I really do not understand why some people fret about the things they do, and there are times when I have little sympathy for their distress.

The point of all this is that if you scored somewhat below average, it does not mean you are a coldhearted person who is incapable of identifying with the feelings of other people. It may be that you, like me, are somewhat selective in how you experience emotional empathy.

22

How Comfortable Are You with Your Mortality?

THE SENSE OF SYMBOLIC IMMORTALITY SCALE

For each of the following statements, circle the number that most corresponds to your feelings, way of seeing things, or way of living at this stage in your life. Please note that the numbers always range from 1 to 7, number 1 indicating strong disagreement with the statement and number 7 indicating strong agreement with the statement. Try to use number 4 ("neutral") as little as possible, since this position indicates absence of judgment in either direction.

> 1 = Strongly disagree
>
> 2 = Disagree
>
> 3 = Slightly disagree
>
> 4 = Neutral
>
> 5 = Slightly agree
>
> 6 = Agree
>
> 7 = Strongly agree

_____ 1. I have developed a personal understanding of existence that helps me to appreciate life fully.

_____ 2. The physical surroundings in which I live are very healthy.

_____ 3. Nothing interesting happens in my life.

_____ 4. I don't have any influence on my surroundings.

_____ 5. I am of no value in the eyes of society.

_____ 6. If I died today, I feel that absolutely no trace or influence of myself would remain.

_____ 7. I participate in the development of many others.

_____ 8. I feel that in spite of my inevitable death, I will always be an integral part of the world.

_____ 9. I feel that I am doing what I want in life.

_____10. I have certain values or beliefs that help me accept or rise above my mortal condition.

_____11. I have the feeling that human nature is doomed to destruction.

_____12. Intimate relationships scare me.

_____13. Once I've decided to do something, I do it with sustained interest.

_____14. I often feel very lonely.

_____15. The eventuality of my death contributes toward giving meaning and structure to my life.

_____16. My sex life contributes greatly to my well-being.

_____17. I have difficulty undertaking new things.

_____18. I feel comfortable in my body.

_____19. My love life brings me joy.

_____20. I feel competent in what I do.

_____21. If I died today, I have the feeling that I would live on in certain people I would leave behind.

_____22. I am full of energy and vitality.

_____23. I am not sure of who I am.

_____24. I am satisfied with my life so far.

_____25. I have good contact with others.

_____26. I feel that I do not use my time well.

Reprinted with the permission of Dr. Jean-Louis Drolet of the Université Laval, Quebec, Canada. For more information see: J. L. Drolet (1990). "Transcending Death During Early Adulthood: Symbolic Immortality, Death Anxiety, and Purpose in Life." *Journal of Clinical Psychology,* 46, 148–60.

SCORING

The score for the following items must be reversed (7 = 1, 6 = 2, 5 = 3, etc.): 3, 4, 5, 6, 11, 12, 14, 17, 19, 23, and 26. After reversing the designated items, add to find your total score.

NORMS

SCORE	PERCENTILE
166	85
149	70
132	50
115	30
98	15

About the Sense of Symbolic Immortality Scale

I admit to being a rather simple, concrete individual. During my college years, I enjoyed discussing the meaning of life into the wee hours of the morning, but once I finished school, began my career, and had children, there did not seem to be much time, or much point, to such discussions. I do believe I have a pretty clear idea of what it takes to make me happy, and it is rather simple. I want my family to be happy and healthy, I like to have an interesting project to work on, and I look forward to rounds of golf with my friends. I say this to help you understand why I do not really grasp the concepts that theorists such as Jean-Louis Drolet, the author of the Symbolic Sense of Immortality Scale, are talking about. This, despite the fact that on my best days, I would receive a very high score on his test and even on my not-so-good days, I would still score above average.

Drolet was interested in the concept of existential anxiety. People who suffer from existential anxiety experience despair and emptiness. They do not find meaning in their day-to-day activities and they feel lost. According to Drolet, these people have not come to terms with their mortality. Death, he has written, is the ultimate given of our existence. While we may push thoughts of our eventual death out of our conscious awareness, the knowledge that we are mortal is always with us. We must achieve, Drolet argues, a personal and authentic awareness of death if we are to live to the fullest and to achieve our human potential. The prospect of our death is a "deadening image," and if we are to find meaning in our life, we must accept its reality, which will then enable us to experience "vitalizing images"—images that energize us and enable us to experience the joy of life.

Drolet, whose research was inspired by philosopher Robert Jay Lifton, has enumerated five modes of experiencing our connection with the world, also called modes of symbolic immortality, that can generate vitalizing images. The first is called the biological mode. This is the sense of continuity we have with our ancestors and our progeny. We feel that we will always carry with us a part of our parents and that our children will always carry with them a part of us. Those with an especially strong sense of this mode can extend this feeling of continuity to their culture, tribe, or nation. They feel they are a part of something larger than themselves and that this larger group provides them with symbolic immortality.

The creative mode comes from the belief that one's contributions to others provide symbolic immortality. The contributions can range from the great (a classic novel or piece of art) to the humble (imparting certain values to one's children or friends). This provides the sense that one's life is worthwhile because its influence will extend beyond death.

The last three modes are pretty abstract, but let me try to briefly describe them The natural mode comes third, and this is characterized by the feeling that one is part of a universe that is eternal and beyond oneself.

Spiritual attainment is the fourth mode, and it involves a personal quest for ultimate meaning and continuity that provides power over death. Spiritual attainment may be found in the notion of life after death, but it can also reflect the abstract sense that death provides release to a higher plane of existence. The final mode of existence is experiential transcendence. This is described as the capacity to lose oneself in the elements and movements of human flow. This state is sometimes associated with feelings of ecstasy and of being fully alive. Drolet wrote that such feelings can be associated with any activity, however mundane, but are most likely to be experienced during exceptional moments, such as when giving birth, having an orgasm, or achieving an athletic or artistic triumph.

I do have misgivings about much of the theory behind Drolet's test, but I believe he has developed a useful and meaningful instrument. Drolet's evidence supported his hypothesis that a sense of symbolic immortality is something we acquire as we grow older and accumulate experience. People in their forties have significantly higher scores than students in their teens and early twenties. Furthermore, he showed that people with high scores on his test did have lower levels of death anxiety and a stronger sense of purpose in their lives. I am sure that people with a high score on this test do find their lives meaningful and purposeful. It is also very possible that people with low scores feel lost and full of despair about their inability to connect with the world around them.

I would question, however, his argument that one must come to "authentically" accept one's mortality in order to find meaning in one's life. I mostly try not to think about my inevitable death. During those times, such as the death of a friend or colleague, when it is impossible not to do so, I feel sheer terror. I hate the thought of dying and find little comfort in the knowledge that my children will remember me and a couple of my books may remain in libraries for a few more years. Nonetheless, I do feel my life has been a rich experience, and other than those moments of terror when the reality of death hits me, I do not believe I suffer from existential anxiety. I suspect that there are different ways of finding meaning and purpose in life and the key is to be free of the barriers that prevent us from connecting with other people or from striving to accomplish our goals. I leave it to you to find the best way to experience your life as meaningful.

23
Do You Like New Experiences?

THE NEOPHILIA SCALE

The following statements sample how people feel about themselves and other people. There are no right or wrong answers. What is important is what you personally believe or feel is true of yourself. Read each statement carefully, then, using the guidelines below, mark how much you agree or disagree with it.

> 5 = Strongly agree
> 4 = Agree
> 3 = Neither agree nor disagree
> 2 = Disagree
> 1 = Strongly disagree

_____ 1. I think there should be less change in our society.

_____ 2. I am uncomfortable when things stay the same for long.

_____ 3. When ordering a meal in a restaurant, I tend to avoid unusual dishes or dishes I have never tasted before.

_____ 4. When I choose where I would like to go for a vacation, I tend to choose unusual or exotic places.

_____ 5. The structure of our society should change less than it does.

_____ 6. People who know me seem to think I am into strange and unusual things.

_____ 7. When I go to see a movie, I tend to avoid "arty" ones.

_____ 8. My tastes in music are unorthodox.

_____ 9. I would rather take a strange but interesting course than a more conventional but useful one.

_____ 10. The style of my clothes is somewhat outlandish.

_____ 11. Acupuncture can do nothing conventional medicine cannot do better.

_____ 12. Pigs can fly.

_____ 13. I would like to be one of the first passengers to go to the moon.

_____ 14. Current sexual mores are too permissive.

_____ 15. The things I laugh at are the things most people think are funny.

_____ 16. More people ought to experiment with "mind-altering" drugs.

_____ 17. Given the chance, I would rather parachute from a plane than go to a ball.

_____ 18. I would not like my boyfriend/girlfriend/spouse to be different from what people expect him/her to be.

_____ 19. I would never like to try eating insects.

_____ 20. I am always thinking of better ways of doing things.

_____ 21. I do not like to take risks.

_____ 22. I sometimes wonder what it would be like to be someone else.

_____ 23. Most people are stuffier than I am.

_____ 24. There is a lot to be said for tradition.

_____ 25. I can understand those who long for "The Good Old Days."

_____ 26. Old friends are the best friends.

_____ 27. I was happier when I was younger.

_____28. I do not believe it is right to pass laws on matters of morals.

_____29. Even when most people do something one way, there is usually a better way if we search for it.

_____30. There is no such thing as an evil person.

_____31. Crime is caused by the situations people find themselves in.

_____32. Changes in sex roles have brought us to a position that is about right.

_____33. The pressures for sexual equality have gone too far.

_____34. I like change.

_____35. Things are changing too much in my life now.

_____36. People should always seek personal growth.

_____37. I often long for the simplicity of the past.

_____38. They don't make things like they used to.

Reprinted with permission of Dr. Iain Walker. For more information see: I. Walker, and K. Gibbins (1989). "Expecting the Unexpected: An Explanation of Category Width." *Perceptual and Motor Skills,* 68, 715–24.

SCORING

Reverse the score (5 = 1, 4 = 2, 3 = 3, 2 = 4, 1 = 5) for the following items: 1, 3, 5, 7, 11, 14, 15, 18, 19, 21, 24, 25, 26, 27, 28, 32, 33, 35, 37, and 38. After completing this step, add your responses to the items.

NORMS

SCORE		PERCENTILE
Men	Women	
140	134	85
133	127	70
125	119	50
117	111	30
110	104	15

About the Neophilia Scale

There are lots of people who have few psychological barriers to overcome. They are relatively free from anxiety and depression, and they have the interpersonal skills to connect with other people. Yet, some of these people are miserable. They have all the resources they need at their disposal and they do not know what to do with them.

Any number of psychologists, to say nothing of philosophers, spiritual leaders, and artists, have suggested what is necessary to have a satisfying, fulfilling life, and I suspect that most of these ideas are valid—for at least some people. The point is, of course, that once we have overcome our barriers to effective functioning, we have to find a solution for finding meaning and happiness that works for us.

While it is impossible for anyone to say what is right for everyone, I do believe that one characteristic that most happy, satisfied people have in common is an appreciation for, and even a desire to have, fresh, new experiences. That is why I included Iain Walker and Keith Gibbins's test to measure neophilia—a love of the new.

Walker and Gibbins were studying the rather esoteric topic of category width (the degree of inclusiveness people use when they place things or concepts into categories) when they serendipitously discovered the role of neophilia. The details are not of importance here, but they found that people who scored high on the Neophilia Scale preferred to concentrate on the "big picture" in life. When collecting information or making judgments, high scorers were likely to make "errors of inclusion." They would rather have too much information than not enough. Low scorers, on the other hand, prefer specific details rather than the big picture and are more likely to make "errors of exclusion." They are motivated to avoid new information that might threaten their preconceived beliefs. Walker and Gibbins reported several more differences between high and low scorers. Compared to their low-scoring peers, high scorers were more accepting of social change, had more unorthodox tastes, were more interested in making personal changes, and were more willing to take risks in order to have new experiences.

Walker and Gibbins did not speculate about the implications of their test for a more general satisfaction with life, but as I suggested earlier, I believe that people with high scores on this scale are more likely to find their lives meaningful and satisfying. My own life experiences have convinced me that an openness to new experiences is critical to giving one's life purpose. I feel extremely fortunate, since my job demands that I learn new things continuously. I am forced to learn the latest developments to be a competent teacher and researcher. And I have enjoyed writing books for the layperson because I never fail to learn much that is new to me in the process.

Most teachers, I suspect, would have a high score on this Neophilia Scale. And the opportunities that the profession provides for satisfying this need for the new is a large part of what makes it so satisfying. But I do know some exceptions. I have had colleagues who felt it burdensome to keep up with changes in the field. Rather than embrace new technology, which always serves to make our jobs easier once we have mastered it, they viewed it as yet another demand on their limited time. As you might guess, these people were not happy. They seemed at least mildly depressed much of the time, and they wondered how they would make it to their retirement date.

While some occupations offer more opportunities to satisfy one's neophilia than others, even those people with the most routine jobs can spend much of their nonworking time expanding their horizons and enriching their lives. I can think of hundreds of examples. One friend did not know anything about soccer until his six-year-old son joined a team. To share his son's interest, he began to read about the sport and volunteered as an assistant coach for his son's second season. His interest lasted longer than his son's, and eventually he began to referee for college games. The travel and the opportunity to meet new people greatly enriched his life.

Another friend knew nothing about financial matters but in her midforties she decided she should begin to save for her retirement. She did not even know what a mutual fund was when she met with personnel to arrange her payroll deduction, so she decided she had better start learning so she could make wise decisions. After reading everything she could find for six months, she began an investment club with her colleagues. After a few years, she became a valued speaker for similar clubs throughout her state.

I hear people complain that their lives are boring, that nothing interesting ever happens to them. But these are the same people who come home every evening, sit themselves down in front of the television, and watch the same old shows night after night. No wonder their lives are tedious! I think the solution to these people's ennui can be found in a Woody Allen movie. He was talking with Annie Hall about relationships when he said they were like sharks—they have to keep moving forward or they would die. I think life is like that too. We have to keep moving forward, we have to learn new things, we have to seek out new experiences. The alternative is too unpleasant to think about.

24

Do You Experience
Moments of Joy?

THE PEAK
EXPERIENCES SCALE

The following statements describe a variety of experiences people have had. Please read each item carefully and indicate if it is "True" or "False" for you.

_____ 1. I have never had an experience that made me extremely happy and, at least temporarily, removed much of my perplexity and confusion.

_____ 2. I have never had an experience that made me extremely happy and, at least temporarily, moved me closer to a perfect identity.

_____ 3. I have had an experience that made me extremely happy and, at least temporarily, made me feel more unique than I usually feel.

_____ 4. I have had an experience that made me feel more unique than I usually feel.

_____ 5. I have had an experience that made me extremely happy and, at least temporarily, caused me to feel that the world was sacred.

_____ 6. I have had an experience that made me extremely happy and, at least temporarily, filled me with surrender.

_____ 7. I have never had an experience that made me extremely happy and, at least temporarily, helped me to totally accept the world.

_____ 8. I have never had an experience that made me extremely happy and, at least temporarily, made me unable to blame or condemn anyone.

_____ 9. I have had an experience that made me extremely happy and, at least temporarily, made me a freer agent than I usually am.

_____10. I have never had an experience that made me extremely happy and, at least temporarily, made me want to do something good for the world.

_____11. I have had an experience that made me extremely happy and, at least temporarily, gave me a glimpse of the purpose that lies behind the events of this world.

_____12. I have never had an experience that made me extremely happy and, at least temporarily, allowed me to realize that the whole universe is an integrated and unified whole.

_____13. I have had an experience that made me extremely happy and, at least temporarily, caused my private, selfish concerns to fade away.

_____14. I have never had an experience that made me extremely happy and, at least temporarily, made me feel very lucky and fortunate.

_____15. I have never had an experience that made me extremely happy and, at least temporarily, gave me a greater appreciation of effortlessness and grace.

_____16. I have had an experience that made me extremely happy and, at least temporarily, gave my whole life new meaning.

_____17. I have never had an experience that made me extremely happy and, at least temporarily, made me incapable of negative emotions, only pity, charity, kindness, and perhaps sadness or amusement.

_____18. I have had an experience that made me extremely happy and, at least temporarily, caused time to seem to stand still.

_____19. I have had an experience that made me extremely happy and, at least temporarily, caused me to feel great kindness toward humanity.

_____20. I have never had an experience that made me extremely happy and, at least temporarily, made me feel as if all my wants and needs were satisfied.

_____21. I have had an experience that made me extremely happy and, at least temporarily, caused me to like and accept everyone.

_____22. I have had an experience that made me extremely happy and, at least temporarily, caused me to perceive the world and others in a more unselfish manner.

_____23. I have never had an experience that made me extremely happy and, at least temporarily, allowed me to realize that everyone has his/her place in the universe.

_____24. I have never had an experience that made me extremely happy and, at least temporarily, helped me to a greater appreciation of uniqueness and individuality.

_____25. I have had an experience that made me extremely happy and, at least temporarily, caused me to feel that the world is totally good.

_____26. I have never had an experience that made me extremely happy and, at least temporarily, helped me to a greater appreciation of necessity and the inevitable.

_____27. I have had an experience that made me extremely happy and, at least temporarily, gave me a greater appreciation of richness.

_____28. I have had an experience that made me extremely happy and, at least temporarily, caused me to perceive the world and others in a more self-transcending manner.

_____29. I have had an experience that made me extremely happy and, at least temporarily, caused me to become disoriented in time.

_____30. I have never had an experience that made me extremely happy and, at least temporarily, made me more accepting of pain than I usually am.

_____31. I have had an experience that made me extremely happy and, at least temporarily, made me feel both proud and humble at the same time.

_____32. I have had an experience that made me extremely happy and, at least temporarily, removed many of my inhibitions.

_____33. I have never had an experience that made me extremely happy and, at least temporarily, helped me to transcend myself.

_____34. I have never had an experience that made me extremely happy and, at least temporarily, gave me a sense of obligation to do constructive things.

_____35. I have never had an experience that made me extremely happy and, at least temporarily, helped me to a greater appreciation of completion and closure than I had before.

_____36. I have had an experience that made me extremely happy and, at least temporarily, made me feel freer than I usually feel.

_____37. I have never had an experience that made me extremely happy and, at least temporarily, involved total listening.

_____38. I have never had an experience that made me extremely happy and, at least temporarily, gave my life new worth.

_____39. I have never had an experience that made me extremely happy and, at least temporarily, caused me to feel that the world is totally beautiful.

_____40. I have never had an experience that made me extremely happy and, at least temporarily, helped me to appreciate beauty to a greater degree than I usually do.

_____41. I have never had an experience that made me extremely happy and, at least temporarily, put me in a state of total visual concentration.

_____42. I have had an experience that made me extremely happy and, at least temporarily, produced greater integration and unity within my personality.

_____43. I have had an experience that made me extremely happy and, at least temporarily, made me very grateful for the privilege of having had it.

_____44. I have never had an experience that made me extremely happy and, at least temporarily, put me in a state of total concentration.

_____45. I have had an experience that made me extremely happy and, at least temporarily, made me feel as if I had everything. I could not think of anything else that I wanted.

_____46. I have had an experience that made me extremely happy and, at least temporarily, reduced my anxiety level greatly.

_____47. I have had an experience that made me extremely happy and, at least temporarily, helped me to appreciate wholeness, unity, and integration to a greater degree than I usually do.

_____ 48. I have never had an experience that made me extremely happy and, at least temporarily, led me to realize that there is a meaningfulness to the universe.

_____ 49. I have never had an experience that made me extremely happy and, at least temporarily, helped me to a greater appreciation of dichotomy-transcendence (seeing opposites as related).

_____ 50. I have never had an experience that made me extremely happy and, at least temporarily, caused me to view the world as totally desirable.

_____ 51. I have never had an experience that made me extremely happy and, at least temporarily, made me more passive toward the world than I usually am.

_____ 52. I have had an experience that made me extremely happy and, at least temporarily, caused me to believe that I could not be disappointed by anyone.

_____ 53. I have never had an experience that made me extremely happy and, at least temporarily, allowed me to view all things, important and unimportant, as nearly equal in significance.

_____ 54. I have never had an experience that made me extremely happy and, at least temporarily, made the conflicts of life seem to disappear.

_____ 55. I have had an experience that made me extremely happy and, at least temporarily, gave me great insight.

_____ 56. I have never had an experience that made me extremely happy and, at least temporarily, caused my perception of the world to become more object-centered (as opposed to self-centered) than usual.

_____ 57. I have never had an experience that made me extremely happy and, at least temporarily, caused me to view others and the world in a more impersonal manner than I usually do.

_____ 58. I have had an experience that made me extremely happy and, at least temporarily, caused me to feel that people are sacred.

_____ 59. I have had an experience that made me extremely happy and, at least temporarily, led me to accept everything.

_____ 60. I have never had an experience that made me extremely happy and, at least temporarily, helped me to a greater appreciation of perfection.

_____ 61. I have had an experience that made me extremely happy and, at least temporarily, allowed me to experience "unitive consciousness."

_____ 62. I have never had an experience that made me extremely happy and, at least temporarily, gave me a glimpse of the "ideal world" that lies behind this world.

_____ 63. I have had an experience that made me extremely happy and, at least temporarily, caused me to become disoriented in space.

_____ 64. I have had an experience that made me extremely happy and, at least temporarily, helped me to view the world in a more detached and objective manner.

_____ 65. I have had an experience that made me extremely happy and, at least temporarily, allowed me to see that individual consciousness is merely an aspect of a total transcending consciousness.

_____ 66. I have never had an experience that made me extremely happy and, at least temporarily, led me to believe that I could die with dignity.

_____67. I have had an experience that made me extremely happy and, at least temporarily, caused me to feel that I didn't even want to justify its worth.

_____68. I have had an experience that made me extremely happy and, at least temporarily, caused me to view the world and others in a more self-forgetful way.

_____69. I have had an experience that made me extremely happy and, at least temporarily, helped me to realize that I could never commit suicide.

_____70. I have had an experience that made me extremely happy and, at least temporarily, helped me to transcend or resolve dichotomies like beautiful versus ugly.

Reprinted with the permission of Dr. Eugene W. Mathes of Western Illinois University. For more information see: E. W. Mathes, M. A. Zevon, P. M. Roter, and S. M. Joerger (1982). "Peak Experience Tendencies: Scale Development and Theory Testing." *Journal of Humanistic Psychology*, 22, 92–108.

SCORING

Your total score is the number of times your responses correspond to the scoring key below:

1. F	9. T	17. F	25. T
2. F	10. F	18. T	26. F
3. T	11. T	19. T	27. T
4. T	12. F	20. F	28. T
5. T	13. T	21. T	29. T
6. T	14. F	22. T	30. F
7. F	15. F	23. F	31. F
8. F	16. T	24. F	32. T

33. F	43. T	53. F	63. T
34. F	44. F	54. F	64. F
35. F	45. T	55. T	65. T
36. T	46. T	56. F	66. F
37. F	47. T	57. F	67. T
38. F	48. F	58. T	68. T
39. F	49. F	59. T	69. T
40. F	50. F	60. F	70. T
41. F	51. F	61. T	
42. T	52. T	62. F	

NORMS

SCORE		PERCENTILE
Men	Women	
61	63	85
56	58	70
50	52	50
44	46	30
39	41	15

About the Peak Experiences Scale

Eugene Mathes and his colleagues at Western Illinois University constructed the Peak Experiences Scale to test elements of Abraham Maslow's theory of personality. If you have ever taken a psychology class, you have heard of Maslow, who was one of the first humanistic psychologists—psychologists who focus on the positive elements of human nature. Best known for his hierarchy of motives, Maslow speculated that once certain basic needs were met, people would then strive to satisfy higher-order needs. Physiological needs are at the bottom of this hierarchy. At the most basic level, people must have food, water, warmth, and during adulthood, sex. Should they satisfy these needs, then they strive to meet safety needs, which include avoiding injury, illness, and physical abuse. Next in the hierarchy are acceptance needs. We want others to like us, to approve of us, to include us, and to love us. Should one feel accepted, then the next step is to satisfy esteem needs. People have a need to feel competent, effective, and useful. They want to feel pride in what they do and the kind of people they are.

At the very top of the hierarchy is self-actualization. People who reach this stage have a need for personal development. They are free from the anxieties and distortions that plague so many of us, and this enables them to be exceptionally accurate in their judgments of other people and situations. Maslow believed that self-actualized people could use their extremely high level of psychological functioning to excel in most any field, including the scientific, the artistic, and even public service. Self-actualized people are not perfect, but they are free from the barriers that prevent many people from reaching their full potential.

Maslow wrote that self-actualized people are especially likely to have what he called peak experiences. These are brief experiences when people transcend ordinary reality and, to use Maslow's terms, perceive "Being or ultimate reality." This allows them to appreciate the beauty, richness, and goodness of life and the universe. Peak experiences are almost always accompanied by feelings of intense joy and happiness. These experiences have a mystical quality, and they have the power of transformation. Maslow argued that such experiences promote even higher levels of psychological functioning.

I do not always completely understand the writings of humanistic psychologists, but I have had a few peak experiences of my own, sometimes in rather mundane circumstances. I still remember the feeling of pure joy at being alive one morning when I was feeding breakfast to my six-month-old son. I have felt overwhelmed by the beauty of the world while on the golf course at sunrise with several of my friends. These are special moments, and despite my inability to grasp all of Maslow's concepts, I do recognize and appreciate the concept of peak experiences.

Maslow did acknowledge that people who had not reached the self-actualization stage could have peak experiences, and that not all self-actualized people had these special moments. People who never have such experiences tend to be more pragmatic, while "peakers" tend to be more poetic and creative. Maslow's contention that having such experiences reflects psychological adjustment has been supported by research psychologists. Compared to those who never have such experiences, peakers are described as more intelligent, assertive, tenderminded, imaginative, self-sufficient, and assertive. They are also less authoritarian and dogmatic, and they experience fewer of the barriers we have discussed in this book. Perhaps most interestingly, peakers were less concerned with material possessions and status, and they were more likely to find life meaningful.

I suspect that having these intensely joyful experiences does provide a rough index of the status of one's mental state. From my experience, such moments are most likely to occur when I am free from any distractions and am generally pleased with the way things are going at the time. Solitude seems to be another helpful ingredient, and several of my experiences have occurred when I've been alone, on a vacation without much to think about except my surroundings. I do not think it is possible to will a peak experience to occur, but it is possible to arrange the circumstances to increase their likelihood.

If you have never had such an experience, it does not

necessarily mean that you have not reached a very high level of psychological functioning. Remember, Maslow reported that not all self-actualized people had such moments. The ability to "peak" does seem to require a certain degree of mysticism. Mathes and his colleagues did report that people whose test scores indicated they were open to self-altering experiences were more likely to have these peak experiences. My hope is that you will have many such moments.

Epilogue
Translating Knowledge into Action

In the Introduction I referred to the 1999 surgeon general's report that concluded that half of all people will experience a psychological disorder at some point in their lives and that a majority of these people will never seek treatment for their problems. While this sounds like a grim statistic, I do believe there is a hopeful explanation.

First, over the years a number of researchers have found that many problems are resolved without professional help. Although I hope you do not use this as justification for inaction, some people experience distress for a few months and either through their own efforts or a change in circumstances, they gradually return to their old selves. An example would be those whose anxiety or depression was caused by a crisis, such as divorce or losing a job. Once the situation is resolved, it may well be that the psychological problem fades away as well. But again, do not suffer patiently, hoping that this will be your experience. Even if you are one of these fortunate people, you can speed the process along considerably by taking an active role in overcoming your barriers.

Second, we have also learned that every community has natural helpers. These people can be found everywhere, and they seem to have a special knack for listening, supporting, and helping their friends and acquaintances. They can be teachers, hairdressers, and yes, even bartenders. Research has shown that for some problems, these natural helpers can be as effective in helping people feel better as are mental health professionals. You may know one of these natural helpers. Do not hesitate to take full advantage of his or her ear. It may be just what you need to overcome your barriers to a better life.

A third possible explanation as to why some people may not seek help from a professional is the increasing availability of high-quality self-help materials. We have always known that there are not enough professional therapists to treat everyone who has a problem, but until recently the profession has done little about it other than lament the need for more psychological services. Over the past decade, a growing number of researchers have developed self-help programs for a variety of problems and collected scientific evidence of their effectiveness. These programs can be found in books, on compact discs, and even on the Internet—a trend I expect will accelerate in the coming years. Indeed, each month several new sites, many of which have been developed by respected clinicians, become available. So, once you have used these tests to identify your barriers, you will be able to find proven self-help materials to help you overcome them.

The key to any attempt to use self-help methods is motivation and persistence. The very fact that you are reading these words is a good indication you have what it takes to overcome your barriers. You are motivated to change, and you are willing to take steps to begin the process.

Once you settle on a strategy for overcoming your barriers, you must be persistent. Change is never easy, and the very nature of psychological problems makes it easier to avoid difficult situations than to confront them. Do not become discouraged the first time you attempt to make some small change and it leaves you feeling worse rather than better. It is something of a cliché (clichés achieve that status because they usually contain a large grain of truth), but you almost certainly will have to feel worse before you can feel better. The road to progress is always bumpy, and you will have your share of dips before you reach your destination. But as long as you maintain a steady course, the odds are excellent that you will make it, that you will overcome your barriers.

If your attempts at self-help do not result in the progress you would like to see, do not hesitate to consult a mental health professional. As the surgeon general's report indicated, there are effective treatments for most problems, and you could almost certainly benefit from utilizing a professional's expertise. Many people can obtain the services of a professional at no cost, or a modest fee. Students can visit their health center or counseling office. Many companies have employee assistance programs for their employees, and most health insurance policies include mental health coverage. Most communities offer mental health services with a sliding scale for fees. Those of you who live near a university or teaching hospital can call their department of psychiatry or psychology and ask about services. Their advanced students see clients for free or, at most, a modest fee. If none of these options is available to you, do not hesitate to call mental health professionals in private practice and ask if they offer a sliding scale for fees. Some will not, but the odds are excellent you could find someone who would see you for a fee you could afford.

The key is not to give up. It can be a tough struggle to change, and there are no guarantees of success. But the odds are in your favor, and as long as you continue to make the effort, the chances are excellent that you can overcome your barriers and have a more satisfying and effective life. I hope this book will be helpful to you in this important endeavor.